*The World
of Young
Herbert Hoover*

Historical books
by Suzanne Hilton

The World of Young Tom Jefferson
The World of Young George Washington
We the People: The Way We Were, 1783–1793
Faster than a Horse: Moving West with Engine Power
Getting There—Frontier Travel Without Power
The Way It Was—1876

The World
of Young
Herbert Hoover

Suzanne Hilton

illustrated by Deborah Steins

Walker and Company
New York

First published in the United States of America in 1987
by the Walker Publishing Company, Inc.

Published simultaneously in Canada by Thomas Allen & Son
Canada, Limited, Markham, Ontario.

Library of Congress Cataloging-in-Publication Data
Hilton, Suzanne.
    The world of young Herbert Hoover.

    Bibliography: p.
    Includes index.
    Summary: Describes the childhood and youth of the first presi-
dent to be born west of the Mississippi River.
    1. Hoover, Herbert, 1874–1964—Childhood and youth—Juve-
nile literature.   2. Presidents—United States—Biography—Juve-
nile literature.   [1. Hoover, Herbert, 1874–1964—Childhood and
youth.   2. Presidents]
I. Steins, Deborah, ill.   II. Title.
E802.H643 1987   973.91'6'0924 [92]   87-6153
ISBN 0-8027-6708-7
ISBN 0-8027-6709-5 (lib. bdg.)

Printed in the United States of America

Contents

118378

Acknowledgments

The author is especially grateful for the unusual and well-documented information provided for this book from:

Edna C. Conley, Librarian of Pawhuska Public Library in Pawhuska, Oklahoma, and

Mildred Mather and Shirley Sondergard, librarians at the Herbert Hoover Presidential Library in West Branch, Iowa.

Extra special thanks are owed to the careful attention to accuracy given by Mr. Dwight Miller, Senior Archivist at the Herbert Hoover Presidential Library, West Branch, Iowa.

1

Little Brown House
on the Prairie

"Boys are very durable. A boy, if not washed too often and if kept in a cool quiet place after each accident, will survive broken bones, hornets' nests, swimming holes, and five helpings of pie."
—Herbert Hoover

A LIGHT IN THE NIGHT meant one of two things. Either someone was sick or someone was being born.

Houses on the Iowa prairie rarely showed a light after darkness. The Quaker families who lived in the small village of West Branch finished all their chores during the daylight hours the Lord provided. No call for wasting the fuel in a kerosene lantern. Night was for resting a weary body.

And yet, light was streaming from the windows of a tiny brown house on Downey Street near midnight on August 10, 1874. Jesse Clark Hoover stood outside, watching the moths play in the unexpected brightness.

Already he had paced a well-worn path between the back porch and the chicken house. The night was hot and the smell of Hulda's garden flowers sweetened the humid air. The rooster, disturbed by the strange light, had crowed at first, but was quiet now. The women, with little concern for Jesse's panic, had sent him outside to wait alone for his second child to be born.

He glanced often at his little son, Tad, sleeping on the floor of the lean-to summer kitchen. Once Jesse strolled across the road to his blacksmith shop, but there was no work he could do there quietly. The entire village would waken with just one clang from his hammer. He wandered back to the small house and pumped a bucket of water, in case it should be wanted. He considered walking across to the simple Quaker meetinghouse, then decided he should not go too far away.

At last he heard Grandmother Minthorn's soft whisper.

"Thee may come in now, Jesse." She spoke in her quiet, Quaker way. All Quakers used "thee" and "thy" in place of "you" and "your" when they spoke to each other.

Jesse sprinted into the small bedroom to find Hulda smiling sleepily and cuddling their second son. They named the baby Herbert Clark Hoover. But he had been born so close to midnight that none of the women present had noticed whether he was born on the tenth or eleventh of August.

Jesse said that little Bertie Hoover could decide on his own birthday when he was older. As soon as he was old enough to understand birthdays, Bertie saw no reason to wait longer than necessary for his special day. He chose to celebrate it on August 10.

The morning after Bertie was born, according to Hulda's sister, Agnes Miles, Jesse Hoover knocked on her door.

"Well, we have another General Grant at our house," the new father announced proudly. "Hulda would like to see thee." General Ulysses S. Grant was then the President of the United States.

Just after little Theodore Jesse Hoover—Tad for short— was born, in 1871, Jesse had paid ninety dollars for two lots along the Wapsinonoc Creek. There, he and his father, Eli Hoover, built a two-room home from boards that had been rafted down the Mississippi River and hauled overland by horse and wagon. For warmth, they stuffed mattress ticking between the boards and eventually covered the walls with paper.

Hulda's mother, Mary Minthorn, made rag rugs to cover the floors. Jesse spread many layers of newspapers under the rugs to keep the bitter prairie winds from blowing through the

floorboards in the winter. Hulda hung straight, heavy curtains at the windows, as much to keep out the cold as to have privacy.

The high double bed where Hulda and Jesse's children were born almost filled the small bedroom. Stored underneath it was a low trundle bed that they pulled out at night for Tad to sleep in. Patchwork quilts, also made by Grandmother Minthorn, were covered by woolen spreads. Against one wall, Hulda put her wedding chest, made for her by an uncle in Detroit. The only clothes closet was fashioned from two upright boards with a curtain across the front for a door. There Hulda hung her few plain gray and brown Quaker dresses.

The larger room in the house had space at one end for two rocking chairs and a lounge that served equally well as a sofa or a spare bed. At the opposite end was a folding table, a dry sink, and the pie safe. Hulda's safe was a movable cupboard for storing food. She kept it indoors in cold weather but moved it out to the lean-to summer kitchen in the spring. Its thin metal doors were punctured with a design of tiny holes so that air could get in the cabinet, but flies and crawling insects could not.

The most important item was the wood-burning cookstove. It also stayed in the lean-to during the summer. But in winter, hooked up to the chimney to draw off the poisonous fumes, its warmth heated both rooms—as long as it was filled with wood every few hours. Jesse heartily disliked getting up three and four times on a cold winter night to add wood to the fire to keep them from freezing in their beds!

The Hoovers had plenty of hot water—in a kettle on the back of the warm stove. And the cold water was always in a bucket by the door with a ladle nearby. Hulda kept a washbasin and huck towel there so her men could wash. The toilet, called a privy, was in a small wooden shed in the backyard. Bertie and Tad were not sure whether they dreaded the privy more in the summer, when it smelled terrible, or in winter, when the icy prairie wind blew straight through it.

Before Bertie was old enough to have memories, Tad began keeping track of family events. Without Tad's stories, Bertie would have remembered very little about their early life.

"The best picnics were when our family went with our aunts and uncles and cousins to the Cedar River," said Tad. "I remember Bertie one time, sound asleep with a big handful of yellow clay on top of his head."

Bertie never tired of hearing about the hornets and how his father had swooped him off his feet and raced to the river bank for a handful of mud after he was stung. Later, still sobbing, Bertie had fallen asleep, the mud a small pyramid on his head.

Around West Branch were dozens of Hoover and Minthorn relations. Grandmother Minthorn, Hulda's mother, was a widow and lived with Uncle Pennington. He made kites for the boys and taught them how to build a rabbit trap. One time Uncle Penn killed a skunk in the chicken house, but not without paying the usual price for making a skunk mad. The boys often laughed at the memory of their tiny grandmother chasing big Uncle Penn out to the cornfield to bury his smelly clothes and take a bath in the creek.

Uncle Laban Miles was married to Hulda's sister Agnes. They had a grocery, a barn to play in, a daughter with golden curls—Cousin Harriett—and a son named Theodore.

Uncle John Minthorn and Aunt Laura moved back to West Branch from Tennessee soon after Bertie was born. They brought a baby girl cousin named Tennessee. Uncle John, a doctor, was the only Quaker the boys knew who had gone to the Civil War. His advice to boys was, "Turn the other cheek once, but if he smites it, then punch him." Uncle John was a dashing figure around the little town. He had a stable of twenty-seven spotted Indian ponies, and Indian Jim Hawkheart took care of the horses.

At Uncle Allen Hoover's farm near West Branch, the boys played with cousins Alice and Walter. And at Uncle Benajah and Aunt Ella Hoover's was Cousin George, who was almost grown-up and allowed to go hunting.

Grandpa Eli Hoover's was a favorite place to go on holidays. Tad never forgot, and he never let the rest of the family forget, about the time Grandmother Hoover made taffy, setting it out in the snow to cool. Their dog stole the taffy, and for days it tugged with its paws to pry out the sticky stuff that was holding its teeth tight together.

"And remember the Pumpkin Wars at Uncle Merlin Marshall's?" Tad prodded Bertie. "He'd stack all his pumpkins up in a great pile. Then he let us carve them into jack-o'-lanterns and arrange them in rows. We pretended they were the enemy. We stamped on them and hacked them up with the corn cutter. Uncle Merlin didn't mind, as long as we picked up all the pieces and put them in the troughs for the cows afterwards."

In cases like the Pumpkin War, Bertie did remember that his part of the glory was limited to the cleaning up afterwards.

Great-grandmother Rebecca Hoover was the oldest Hoover relation. She had raised nineteen children, although not all of them were her own. Some were orphans, like Emma and Annie Miles, who lived with her when Bertie was growing up. Rebecca Hoover was full of stories. The Hoover family had once lived in North Carolina, she told the boys, but they could not live with slavery. The Hoovers had freed their slaves and moved to Iowa, where no man kept other men in bondage. For years the Hoovers and Minthorns helped slaves to escape. Uncle John Minthorn was a skillful driver of fast horses. No one ever overtook the team he drove for the underground railroad that carried slaves to freedom.

The Minthorns were friends of abolitionist John Brown. One day Brown told the Minthorns he planned to attack a government arsenal at Harpers Ferry. They tried to persuade him to find peaceful ways to free slaves, but he did not listen. A young Quaker from West Branch rode with Brown's men to Harpers Ferry. When they were captured, he was hung with John Brown.

On Sundays, which the Quakers, or Friends, call "First Day," the Hoovers all went to meeting. Tad sat with his father on the men's side. While he was small, Bertie went with his mother through the women's door, but soon he was allowed to sit with his father and Tad. Between the two groups was a wooden partition that was kept open, except in the monthly meetings, when it was closed so the men and women could conduct their business independently.

Quaker meetings are silent, unless a member feels that he or she is moved to speak. Children learn very early to sit still, or they will be carried into the "cry room" with the other babies. Hard as it was to sit quietly, Bertie knew his big brother would tease him fiercely if he had to be taken out with the babies.

The men and women elders sat on benches facing the congregation. A small wriggling boy could not even count his toes, turn to gaze over the partition, or look at a book. About all small boys could do, said Tad, was watch flies in the sun, listen to the birds outside, or notice when Mr. Pearson fell asleep and wonder how soon Elder Jepson would stir him up. One day a swarm of Isaac Walker's bees flew in the open door and settled in the rafters. Not one of the grown-ups stirred, but many of the children had to be shushed.

As soon as he was tall enough, Tad spent his time in meeting staring over the partition at Millie Branson. He prayed for his freckles to go away so Millie would like him.

The children often wondered how the head man knew when the meeting was over, because there was no clock. But after what seemed like hours, one of the head men facing the congregation would "break the meeting" by shaking hands quietly with the man on his left. Then everyone shook hands and left for home.

A few years before, the meeting had divided into two groups because the older people did not approve of the "frivolous" ideas of the younger people. The younger friends wanted to have music and sometimes use the meetinghouse for nonreligious events.

"Music?" said Aunt Hannah, one of the elders. "This edifice dedicated to God might even become a the-ay-ter!"

Hulda could not find it in her heart to agree. She loved to sing and saw no reason why the Lord could not be praised with prayerful music. When she was sixteen, her father had died, and Hulda had shocked the meeting when she felt moved to sing a hymn at his funeral. Some older Friends had even walked out. Now there were two Quaker meetings in the small town—one of older people that was very strict, and one that the young Hoovers attended, which sometimes had music.

Bertie's first memory was of his father's forge, possibly because he had stepped barefoot one day on a hot piece of metal that had dropped on the dirt floor. His father dipped his injured foot in cold water and wrapped a bandage soaked in linseed oil around the burn. Tad, whose memory of childhood events was much better than Bertie's, claimed that he was the one who had stepped on the hot metal. Bert's foot scar, said Tad, was from stepping on a hayfork in Uncle Allen's barn. All his life Bertie insisted that he also had "the brand of Iowa" on his foot.

Jesse was tall and thin, not so muscular as George Hill or Judson Brundage, the other blacksmiths in town. Like his father, Jesse had an inventive sort of mind. He liked designing tools the farmers needed and putting together agricultural machinery.

Jesse had a heart condition, but not even Dr. Minthorn knew exactly how to treat it. Hulda worried when he delivered heavy machinery to his customers out on the prairie, especially when the blowing winds made the temperature drop far below zero. But Jesse just laughed at her fears. He had so little spare time in his day that he could not afford the luxury of worrying about anything.

Both Bertie and Tad were "croupy," although Tad was now outgrowing this childhood disease. Some nights a "croupy" child would go to bed in perfect health. But then, in the wee hours of the morning, the dreaded coughing, whooping sound would be heard as the croup came on. Hulda had known young children to die because they could not breathe with the croup.

One terrible morning Tad watched silently while his little brother was slowly strangling with the croup. Hulda paced the floor, alternately patting Bertie's back to loosen the congestion and rocking to comfort him. Jesse had fled down the road to find Uncle John Minthorn. When he found that the doctor was still out on a night call, he knocked on other doors, bringing into the dark night a parade of aunts and Grandmother Minthorn.

As they filed into her house, Hulda searched their faces for some sign of encouragement. Laura Minthorn said Indian Jim Hawkheart had ridden out to find the doctor.

Grandmother Mary Minthorn took charge of the battle and ordered water put on the stove to raise a steam. She called for goose grease and onion poultices on Bertie's throat. They tried giving him syrup of ipecac to make him vomit. Nothing worked.

My brother is stretched out on a high table on pillows, Tad wrote later in his memoirs. *Parents, aunts, and cousins are working over him with various household remedies, running to and fro . . . Finally the mother gives up and the father comforts her, and it comes to me that my brother is dead.*

Then suddenly there was a noise on the road outside. Grandmother Minthorn ran out quickly to tell Dr. Minthorn that little Bertie had gone.

But the doctor did not accept defeat easily. He snatched Bertie, turned him upside down, and gave him a few heavy pats that made the women wince. He tried a few other things that Tad could not remember, then put his mouth to Bertie's and blew breath into his lungs. Bertie's eyes opened wide, and he squalled.

"God has a great work for that boy to do. That is why he was brought back to life," pronounced Grandmother Minthorn as soon as she could speak.

2

Adventures and
Great Undertakings

"Boys love to trade things. They'll trade fish hooks, marbles, broken knives and snakes for anything that is priceless or worthless."
—Herbert Hoover

"THERE'S NOT ROOM ENOUGH in this house to swing a cat," said Jesse one day. A baby sister, Mary, called "May," had been born two years before, and the boys seemed always underfoot. Hulda had organized a young people's prayer meeting that crowded into the house on Saturdays, and she too felt the house must be shrinking.

In 1878 Jesse sold the blacksmith shop and cottage to George Hill, and the Hoovers moved for a while into a house next to Uncle Laban Miles's grocery. Tad and Bertie called it "the house where we had the mumps." Then one day in March, Jesse came home from an auction with a surprise.

He had bought a house on the corner of Downey and Cedar streets for $140. Like most of the neighboring Iowa homes, it was surrounded by trees, with large maples in front. Hulda and the boys called it "The House of the Maples." Much work was needed before they could move in, but Jesse promised them luxuries they had never had—ingrain carpets and a modern stove.

The yarn of an ingrain carpet was dyed before the rug was woven. It would not fade in the sun or turn a strange color when it got older. And to think of owning a modern stove that kept an even temperature and did not need to be fed with wood constantly made Hulda's eyes sparkle with pleasure. They moved in on May 27, 1879.

The House of the Maples was what eight-year-old Tad, using a forbidden slang word he had learned from an older boy, called a "boss" house. The boys, with baby May tagging along behind, noisily toured the four rooms of the new house.

One room downstairs was a combination kitchen and dining room. The other room was a real parlor with a new lounge for guests to sit on, lace curtains, and a whatnot shelf. Hulda warned that the new ingrain carpet was to be treated with great respect by small children with dirty shoes. Upstairs were two bedrooms. Bertie thought having a barn in the backyard was "boss," but he was careful to use the word only with Tad.

The boys missed watching the huge roaring fire in Jesse's blacksmith shop. They liked the hammer ringing on the anvil and the sparks that showered down like Fourth of July sparklers under the control of their father. Now Jesse had a new shop in the village, where he sold everything from lightning rods and sewing machines to wagons, plows, cultivators, and barbed wire.

Jesse had bought a barbing machine, and now he could fasten "the Norwegian barb" onto new wire. Farmers came from miles around to buy Hoover's barbed wire. Other wire rusted and then the fences sagged, but Jesse Hoover's wire was dipped in a tank of hot tar to make it rustproof.

Bertie was five on the December day he decided to make a scientific experiment at the shop. Outside, Jesse had heated a huge cauldron of tar to coat the fence wire. As it bubbled thickly, Bertie wondered what might happen if he threw a small, flaming stick into the tar. His curiosity was satisfied at once.

"Much smoke and a big scare," screamed the newspaper headline the next week. "Saturday afternoon a cauldron of tar which J.C. Hoover was heating for a coating for fence wire took fire and immediately great clouds of fire and smoke were sent up, causing much excitement among our people. Everybody with buckets in hand rushed pell mell for the scene of the conflagration which was midway between Hoover's agricultural house and Rummels & White's meat market. A copious application of water soon quieted the fire which caused no damage other than the destruction of the cauldron of tar."

No one knew who or what had caused the fire to roar into the sky. One book about Hoover says he had his first and only spanking that day when his father found out. But Tad says that Bertie told no one but him about it—and then only long after they were both grown up.

Jesse's farm machinery was delivered to him in pieces, and he was the only man in town who could put them together. He delivered the heavy machinery in snow, rain, or sweltering sun, usually staying a few days to show the customer how to run the new machine. Hulda knew how dangerous some of the machines could be. Her brother, Dr. Minthorn, often had to amputate some farmer's hand after he had caught it in a threshing machine.

Hulda had never been able to bake a proper cake in the old woodstove because it would not keep an even heat. Now she practiced baking in her shiny, modern cooking stove before making a special cake for Great-grandmother Rebecca Hoover's seventy-ninth surprise birthday party in November.

Quakers did not have lavish, big parties, listing all the birthday presents in the newspaper the following week, the way some West Branch people did. But Rebecca's party made the newspaper anyway. Most of her nineteen children, dozens of grandchildren, and a large supply of great-grandchildren made it a special occasion for the bright-eyed old lady who had come to West Branch as a pioneer before there was even a town.

It was lucky that Rebecca's party was on a bright, sunny day, because a real photographer came all the way from Iowa City to take their picture, and he needed sunlight to make a photograph. Hulda held up baby May, and Jesse stood in the back row holding Bertie. With no one to hog-tie him, Tad climbed a tree. None of them said "cheese" or smiled, because they did not want to look frivolous. Instead, each one said "prune" or "prism." Then they all held their breaths for the seconds it took for the picture to be recorded on the glass negative.

The Hoovers, like all Quakers, wanted their children to be well-schooled. But just learning to read and write was not enough to suit the Minthorns. Their children must have a college education, if possible.

Joel and Hannah Bean had started the first Quaker school in the town. When people of other religions moved in, the Quaker school became the public school, although the Quaker children still went to the meetinghouse at 10:00 A.M. every Fourth Day (Wednesday) for meditation. Because of the Quaker schooling, the children of West Branch had a better education than many children who lived in large eastern cities. The little village even had a high school in 1877, when most country children were lucky to learn reading, writing, and cyphering. Only ten miles away in Iowa City was a college, where Hulda had studied one semester to be a teacher. She was determined that her children would go to college.

West Branch also had a Mission School, where one hundred Indian boys and girls from tribes all over the Plains had come to learn reading, writing, farming, and housekeeping, so they could live in the white man's world.

In October, Tad and Bertie went with their father to see the "Indian train" at the railroad station. Six of the smartest boys from the Mission School were leaving for the new government school for the education of Indians in Carlisle, Pennsylvania. Already on the train were a hundred Indian boys from several Plains tribes.

After the Civil War, many Quakers from West Branch had gone south to help poor white and black people rebuild their lives. Others, like the Miles and Minthorns, had gone west to help the Indians. The year the Hoovers moved into the

House of the Maples, Dr. John Minthorn and Aunt Laura moved to Arkansas City with Cousin Tennie and their baby, Benjamin Bruce. Uncle John was now the doctor for the Nez Perce and Ponca Indians.

Laban Miles, Aunt Agnes, and Cousin Harriett had moved to Oklahoma, where Uncle Laban was the Indian agent for the Osage and Kaw Indians. Many times he came back to visit, bringing Indian boys and girls to the Mission School.

Hulda was sick the first winter in the new house, and to keep their house warm, Jesse bought a heating stove that burned coal. He built a small shed to store the coals in, but Hulda turned it into a "washhouse." At the end of May she wrote her sister Agnes in Oklahoma:

"We have a new fence all around the lot. Jesse moved the coal house out to the fence by the well. I have mother's old cookstove fixed up in it so I can wash out there. We have now got a nice comfortable little home and I feel thankful and happy every day that we have so many comforts."

Hulda was deeply religious. She taught her children to give thanks for all their comforts with a silent grace at every meal. After breakfast each day, either Hulda or Jesse read from the Bible, said a short prayer, and ended with a silent meditation. When the children learned to read, they took turns reading the Bible stories. Bertie had read the entire Bible by the time he was ten years old.

Excitement in West Branch was of the homemade kind. October was corn-husking time. What could be dull work was livened up with a corn-husking party. Most of the corn was yellow, but when a husker opened one that was red, he could kiss any girl at the party.

Spring through fall, the townspeople had dances, ice cream sociables, and "the best music ever," usually played on man-dolins or banjos at Bean's Hall. The nighttime events were usually scheduled during the full moon, because there were no street lights and people needed the moon to light their way home. The Quakers did not usually show up at such public events, because they considered them a waste of valuable time. However, in the summer, when there were concerts in the town park's band pavilion, several Quakers coincidentally were doing their shopping in town just when the concerts began.

Adults of more severe tastes might stop by at Hulda Hoover's for a meeting of the Women's Christian Temperance Union to hear an essay on the evils of Demon Rum or to debate how to make the government stop the sale of liquor.

Crime in West Branch was handled swiftly, without the help of a policeman. A boy caught stealing apples from a farmer's orchard was told on the spot that he was a criminal. An adult made the boy write a formal letter of apology to the person who owned the apple tree, offering to work until the apples that he had stolen were paid for. Mr. Wickersham, editor of the town's weekly newspaper, fought crime in his own way with notices like these:

"The person who took those odd gloves at James Bean's dry goods store might have saved time and trouble by asking the clerk to wait on him when he came back the second time and took the mates . . ." and

"If those young fellows who participated in that indecent and grossly immoral affair up the railroad the other night don't look a little out, we will treat them to some free advertising, giving their names in full. We trust that they will heed the warning and save themselves from an exposure of their criminal and indecent actions. . . ."

Boys had to be kept busy every second, some of the old Quakers warned the Hoovers. They would be sorry, said Uncle John Minthorn, for buying the oil cookstove and the coal burner, instead of stoves that burned wood and needed to be refilled every few hours.

"Keep the boys tired," said Uncle John. "Then they won't have the energy to get into trouble like those boys along the railroad track."

But Hulda wanted their children to have a chance to fish the Iowa streams, roam in the woods along the river banks, and see the mystery of food growing out of the rich prairie soil. They each had chores to do every day, but after that she hoped they would enjoy some great childhood adventures.

Naturally, the boys agreed. They did not want to be like the banker's son, Bert Chambers, whom they called "the great white slave." Chambers was the best baseball pitcher in town, but he had so many chores to do that the rest of the team had to help him finish his work before he could play an hour with them.

Most boys—never girls—played baseball after chores on a

Saturday. The game was much more popular in West Branch than football, particularly with the Quaker parents. When the older children began playing football at school, their parents complained that the principal must be conniving with the shoemakers in town to destroy good shoes so they could not be handed down to the younger children in the family.

Jesse showed his sons how to fish with a willow pole, a piece of butcher's string for the line, and a hook that cost a penny. He made sleds for them with iron runners and painted the boys' names on the wood. But the homemade sleds were slow on Cook's Hill, where they could never compete with the slick new "coasters" owned by the older boys. Tad and Bertie both managed to trade theirs for coasters by bragging to the owners of the fast sleds that their handmade ones were "the only ones in the whole world like these."

The boys explored the Burlington, Cedar Rapids, and Northern railroad tracks, and especially the rocks used for ballast. Some of the rocks were coral from some mysterious, ancient inland sea. Bertie took home fossils, bits of blue "birds-eye" marble, agate pebbles, and petrified wood pieces. But his mother never invited him to display them on the precious whatnot shelf in the parlor.

He found out why one day when he had a bad toothache and his mother took him to see Dr. Edward Walker, the dentist. Walker also had a stone collection, but his were shiny like jewels. When Bertie exhibited his stones, they always had to be freshly licked because they looked best when wet.

"I polished them on a grindstone to make them stay smooth and shiny," Dr. Walker laughed when Bertie asked if he licked them. "You're welcome to come and see them any time, Bertie."

Bertie may have begun primary school before he was six years old, because in June of 1880 the census taker said both he and Tad had already been to school that year. Lizzie Chandler, his first teacher, remembered that Bertie arrived for his first day with a new slate bordered in red felt.

First grade was known as the C grade of Primary School. B grade was like second grade, and A grade was third. Next came Intermediate School, with C, B, and A grades, now called fourth, fifth and sixth grades. Grammar school was the same as seventh and eighth, and high school followed.

Just before election day in November 1880, Jesse took his sons to a torchlight parade. Since there was only one Democrat in all of West Branch, the "hurrahs" were directed toward the Republican choice for President of the U.S., James A. Garfield. The shouts of the voters, the homemade signs they carried, and especially the torches that lit up Main Street were memories that Bertie could recall without Tad's help. A very tired Bertie remembered being carried that night on his father's strong shoulders.

A few weeks later, Jesse was sicker than Hulda had ever seen him. All the relations who were near came to help, but Hulda's sister, Agnes Miles, and brother, Dr. Minthorn, were far away in Indian country.

The new doctor called Jesse's sickness "rheumatism of the heart" and said Hulda had best send the children to relatives at once. Did he mean Jesse was so very sick? Hulda protested. Her husband was only thirty-four years old. But the doctor looked away from her pleading eyes. Jesse had a diseased heart, probably caused by exposure and hard work when he was young. Dr. Minthorn had once told that to the new doctor. Before Jesse was sixteen, he always got up long before day, curried the horses and harnessed them, ate in a hurry so he could get the thrashing machine humming before sunup, and then stood all day in a cloud of dust, and worked until after dark.

Hulda kept baby May at home and sent the boys off to visit Uncle Benajah Hoover, Aunt Ella, Great-Grandmother Rebecca, and Cousin George, who was twelve. They were still there on December 13, 1880, when a rider came to take them home. Jesse had died that morning.

The Quaker funeral was meant to be comforting. The women

of the family filled the house with a quiet strength and plenty of good food for all the guests who came to call. Hulda felt moved to sing Jesse's favorite hymn, but the life had gone out of her eyes. The three children clung to each other, understanding that they had lost their father but sensing that in some way they had also lost the mother they knew.

"It was many years before I could say the words 'my father,' " said Tad later. "Hugging these griefs too close in silence made them sink too deeply into our hearts. It would have been better if we could have talked about the fun times that we had with him instead."

3

Changing Days and Indian Ways

"The world is so full of boys that it's impossible to touch off a firecracker, strike up a band, or pitch a ball without collecting a thousand of them."

—Herbert Hoover

HULDA AND HER CHILDREN were not the only Iowans who thought the winter of 1880–81 was unusually long and cold. Snow lay on the ground for three months, though usually only a few days in winter were good enough for sleighs and sled riding. In March, the northbound train was snowed up at the station, and twenty passengers crowded into Nathaniel Crook's small West Branch hotel, clamoring for rooms.

The boys took May to Cook's Hill to go sled riding on their coasters. But like all the other girls, May insisted on sitting up on the sled, guiding it with her heels. Finally her brothers gave up.

"We looked upon it as a limitation of her sex," Tad wrote, "as the regular and proper posture was to lie flat on the belly, heels high, and toes pointed down to guide."

Hulda and Benajah Hoover tried to make sense out of Jesse's finances. Many people owed money to Jesse, but not all the debts could be collected. He had trusted everyone, and he often sold his goods to a poor farmer who paid him with butter, eggs, chickens, and sausage. Not enough money was left to pay Jesse's business debts, so Hulda had to decide what to sell.

Benajah bought the small shop and tried for a few years to sell the buggies, sleighs, wagons, sewing machines, and farm tools that Jesse had been so proud to display.

Hulda kept the house with the maple trees in front, one cow, two pigs, a dark bay horse and a light bay mare, a wagon, the oil stove, her mother's cookstove, a sewing machine, six chairs, the feather beds, the lounge and whatnot shelf, a washing machine (worth fifty cents), a wringer, the pie safe, and some pictures. The beloved ingrain carpet was probably sold, because a few years later the old rag carpets were back on the floor.

Fun times were over for Hulda. She found peace and comfort in her religion. In a few years she became such a valuable speaker that her meeting made her a Quaker minister. She was often called away from home to speak at Quaker meetings in other towns. Then the children stayed with loving relations who could not always afford the extra mouths to feed. At least Tad was old enough to help pay his board at his uncle's by milking the cow, hoeing the garden, picking apples, and splitting wood.

Hulda's main goal was to keep her family together. If that meant doing without an ingrain carpet, she was happy to part with it. The small family was not poor, but they would have to be careful. They had a warm house, a garden to supply fresh food, and a sewing machine to make the children's clothes. Hulda owned a few dresses, skirts, a coat, a wool winter bonnet and a summer one, and one oilcloth coat for rain. Five hundred dollars were left to pay all other expenses for a year, but even from that money Hulda managed to put some away for the children's education.

Bertie and Tad tried to earn money. Thompson Walker paid them five cents for every two quarts of strawberries they picked. Bertie ate several of his and spilled some, but Tad earned seven dollars, which bought him new clothes for the coming winter. That was high finance. Their usual wages were one penny for every hundred potato bugs picked off the plants.

In the summer, Hulda took the three children on visits to their Hoover and Minthorn relations. But it was hard to get away from sadness. At Uncle Merlin Marshall's, three of their cousins had just died of diphtheria. Aunt Rebecca Price had just lost her husband. Once, on a visit to Aunt Esther's, the children were surprised to hear their mother laugh—the women were making decorations out of small shells pressed into putty. They laughed again when they saw Bertie's newest collection. He had nestled together three dozen of the crookedest sticks he could find.

Some days Hulda was exhausted from acting as both mother and father to the children.

"The children are trying to clean up the yard today," she wrote her mother one day in March. "I cannot write when there is a racket, and if I were to put down the times 'Mama' was said, it would fill the sheet. The children appreciate Grandmother's letter and when they get so I can settle them long enough, they will write . . . I have tried often to get Bertie to write, but he always says he can't write good enough."

Bertie at age nine was already quiet and shy, as he would be all his life. But Tad, in a hurry to become a man now that he was almost twelve, was leaving nothing untried. Tad learned to smoke cigars behind Uncle Davis Hoover's barn. He read forbidden books and a magazine borrowed from Cousin George Hoover called *The Youth's Companion*. Quakers did not allow their children to read fiction or "imaginary" stories, like those found in *The Youth's Companion*, or in books like *Tom Sawyer* or *Ivanhoe*.

Tad climbed to the top of a tree to rob a hawk's nest, then ripped his britches trying to retreat while the hawk clawed the top of his head. He and his friends snitched apples, which they hid in a secret place along the railroad tracks. Bertie knew that Tad and his friends often hopped onto moving freight cars. But that summer of 1882, the sport suddenly lost its popularity. Walter Meadows, a boy Bertie's age, slipped and fell under the wheels of a freight train.

"He was ground to pieces," Tad said, suddenly realizing that the accident might have happened to his own brother.

No one, not even Bertie, recalled exactly which year Aunt Agnes Miles came to take Bertie to live for nine months on the Osage Reservation in Indian Territory. The most likely time was from spring until the fall opening of school in 1882. Hulda wanted to send her son off with a nice new suit, but money was needed in too many other places. Besides, he would be needing another when he returned for school in the fall. Then, she promised Bertie, they might even talk about buying his first long trousers.

Bertie, dressed in knee pants and gray coat, hugged his mother and climbed aboard the train with Aunt Agnes. They rode to Kansas City and changed to another train that went to Coffeyville, Kansas. From there Aunt Agnes told him, they would ride by wagon to the agency. Perhaps they rode in the new side-spring top buggy that Uncle Laban had just bought for $175. It had a leather top with rubber curtains to use if it rained. Uncle Laban had had it custom-made with one-inch genuine steel axles to withstand the terrible roads in Indian country.

A pair of government mules pulled them. In spite of cluckings and slapping of reins, the mules moved just as they pleased over the bumps. What had looked like a road out of Coffeyville soon disappeared. Only the Indian driver, who had made the trip many times with Uncle Laban, knew which path to follow across shallow streams and over scrub trees. Sometimes, when the buggy bounded and Bertie was sure only one wheel was touching ground, Aunt Agnes had to hold him in.

Hours later they climbed one last hill and stopped. Uncle Laban's house looked huge, with walls nine inches thick to keep out the summer heat. The next day Bert was given a quick tour from basement to attic by his cousins Harriett, who was about ten, Theodore, who was six, and Blanche, four.

Laban Miles had been the Indian agent since July 1878. The Osages had come to love and trust him like a brother and loved his wife, Agnes, just as deeply. When Laban first came to the reservation, the government had given certain lands to each of several tribes. The Osages, Kaws, and Quapaws were to stay west of the ninety-sixth meridian. The Cherokees were to stay east of that invisible line, on land that the Osages said their fathers had once owned.

Indians had no maps with meridian lines drawn on them. They saw only that the land given to the Cherokees was fine for farming and grazing cattle. The land given to the Osages was high, rocky, and valueless. Rainwater poured down ravines, leaving no drink for their ponies and cattle. The Osages even had to ask their Great White Father in Washington for permission to go on a buffalo hunt. Laban Miles wrote thousands of letters and made many trips to the East to plead for the Osages.

In 1881, Miles organized the Osages to form their own constitution. They governed themselves and made their own laws. A white man was allowed in the territory only long enough to do business. Laban saw to it that the whiskey peddlers were not allowed in at all. He drilled wells where he found good water at the bottom of the hills. Wells drilled at the top of hills brought only saltwater, so he built stone storage towers to supply the reservation with safe drinking water.

When Bertie arrived, Laban had built sawmills to cut the wood for new houses. Each Indian was to have 160 acres, fenced in, and a small, one-story frame house with two doors and two windows. Some of the "blanket" Indians still preferred living in the old way and rented their new houses to other men. The Osage Agency was a tiny village with one government building, the agent's home, two Indian council houses, two stores, and a large schoolhouse.

Bertie and his cousins went to a small subscription school in the town. But sixty Quapaws, Osages, and half-breed boys and girls went to the Osage Friends School. Benjamin Miles, the father of Uncle Laban, was the principal. Many of the Indian pupils could not read or write English. From 8:30 A.M.

until lunch, they had reading, writing, arithmetic, and geography. For three hours every afternoon, the boys studied gardening, wood-chopping, butchering, and milking, and helped with the general work about the school building and laundry. The girls spent the same hours learning to wash, iron, sew, and do housework.

At dinner one night Grandpa Benjamin Miles said that a missionary had visited the school that day to find out how well they had succeeded in making good Christians of the Indian children.

"What was your scripture lesson about today?" asked the missionary, knowing very well they had heard the story about Ananias and Sapphira, his wife. The Indian children had all answered together.

"Ananias set fire-a to his wife."

Bertie and Theodore Miles learned to make bows out of Osage orangewood, build small camp fires Indian-fashion, and make traps to catch small animals. They found pieces of a soft stone called "keel" that they could use to write and draw pictures in red. Although they often visited a place the Indian children called "Panther cave," they never saw a panther. Bertie had never known such freedom. Forever after, the outdoors was a place of peace and happiness for him.

He loved the Indian legends he heard every night at bedtime. The Miles children had never been allowed to read or hear any stories that made Indians look bad or mean, and the legends were filled with Indian beliefs and traditions. One of their favorite stories was about the Osage Indian called Pawhuska. Long ago, fighting with the Shawnees, this Indian had tried to scalp an elderly military man who was wearing a white wig. The Indian raised his scalping knife and the man's hair came off! Such a scalp must have magic in it. The white man escaped while the Indian attached the magic scalp to his own scalp lock. He never went into battle without it, certain that it would protect his own life as it had the white man's. Forever after, he was called Pawhu (hair)—Skah (white). Some day,

Uncle Laban added, he hoped to name a town after the Indian Pawhuska.

Aunt Agnes was always very nervous around Pay Day. June was the time the Indians came to collect their money from the Great White Father in Washington. But Indians wanted "hard money," not checks, from the government. So they came to the agency and set up their skin tepees and waited for Uncle Laban to arrive from the town with their pay.

A few days before, Uncle Laban had to travel to Independence City, Kansas, "in the states," to collect the hard money. Often he went alone because, he told Aunt Agnes, robbers were more likely to become suspicious if he had several men or armed guards with him. Usually, Aunt Agnes insisted he take some Osages with him.

On the way home with the money one day when six Indian guards rode with him, Uncle Laban felt a fear that he said was "like a sharp pain." The zigzag trail ahead led to a ravine, thick with trees. The party stopped to rest the mules a few minutes. Then he whispered to them that he had changed his plans. They all turned back a few miles and took a different road. Uncle Laban learned later from a local sheriff that a large gang of bandits had been waiting for him up the hill.

On Pay Day, a helper called out the name of each Indian, one at a time. When an Indian's name was called, he came forward and touched the end of Uncle Laban's pen. Laban wrote the Indian's name and handed him his money. Then the Indians left. But often they left behind their tepees, and the white children played in them.

Some of the 642 Osage families on the reservation used only Indian names, like Show-moh-li-Ke-tompe (Stole a dog and looked at it), Wah-ho-tah-wah-nah-she (Took away the guns), Moh-ses-kah-no-pe (Two dollars), and Nun-tea-wah-hu (Gentle heart). Others kept their Indian names private and used English names they had chosen, like Black Horse Rider, Man Alone, Frank Corndropper, Prince Albert, Bacon Rind, Knee Striker, Big Nose, and No Sense.

In the fall of 1882, "Bertie Hoover" was listed in the first year of C grade in the Intermediate Department back home in West Branch. He was wearing his first long trousers. School began at 9:00 A.M. with a reading from the Bible. At noon most of the children went home for lunch hour, although many times Tad and his friends showed off by going to Crew's Grocery, where they could get dried herrings, cheese, and crackers for three cents.

Bertie found he was good in arithmetic and geography, but he hated having to write compositions in language class. Nothing, however, was as terrifying as the literary exercises held every Friday afternoon. Then, every student had to give a speech or recite a poem in front of the class. Four o'clock never came soon enough to save Bertie from this weekly torture.

Almost everyone at school had an autograph book, and Bertie liked to think of poems to write when he was asked. Older folks wrote dreary notes, like "Be cheerful and contented with your lot," or "In memory's golden casket, drop one pearl for me." Children with no imagination just copied, like one boy who wrote in Addie Colip's autograph book: "In meries goldn casket drok one perl for me." When Addie asked Bertie to sign her book, he gave her one of his best creations: "Let your days be days of peas . . . slip along as slick as greese."

Benjamin and Elizabeth Bean Miles were in charge of the Mission School for Indian children. The summer of 1883 they asked Tad and Bertie to be special friends to three orphaned Indian boys who were to stay all summer in West Branch. Two of the boys, named Miles and Townsend, were full-blooded Osages. The third, Jasper, was a half-breed, and "a born leader" in the boys' eyes.

Both Indians and whites learned many things that summer. The boys built two permanent wickiups in a hazel thicket to use as a meeting place. The paths that Jasper led them over kept far away from farmhouses, winding down stream beds, through fields of high corn, and along fences. In return for

lessons in making bows and arrows and shooting small game, the Hoover boys showed the Indians how to use a slingshot. Not a rabbit, dove, or chicken was safe to venture out in the open that summer. The Osages always built a small fire and roasted the day's catch on the spot—which Tad admitted to be a good idea, especially when the roasted dinner one day was Mattie Larsen's chicken.

Money problems never did go away, although the children never felt poor. All their friends worked to earn money. Nothing was ever thrown away. In every home clothes were cut down for younger children, and when they became ragged, they were made into rugs.

Once Hulda wrote her mother, "You will laugh at my poverty if I tell you I could not scratch up enough to pay my postage—but it has been even so—I have made poor out collecting this winter so have been kind of short some times."

West Branch was changing. Many of the Quakers had sold their farms at a good profit for fifty dollars an acre. They moved farther west, where they could buy land at five dollars an acre, and started all over, even though it meant the whole family would "have to harness to the work pretty smartly."

Almost all the Hoover and Minthorn relatives moved farther west in the three years after Jesse died. They all invited Hulda to visit for several months with her children, or to find a job teaching school near them. She wrote her mother she could not decide.

"Won't you give me your best advice? . . . I want to do what is best for me and the little ones. Oh how much I have longed today for some one to tell me what is best to do."

Loneliness did not keep Hulda from doing what she considered her duty. When the women from the temperance union were angry about the liquor that now flowed freely in West Branch, they decided it was time to put up a fight.

Bertie remembered going with his mother to the polls in Springdale one election day when the temperance women came prepared to make their state prohibit the selling of liquor. Each woman brought baskets of home-baked goodies and set them up on long tables. As the voters walked to the polling place, the women held out plates of the delicious food with one hand. In the other hand, each lady handed a voter a pledge to sign saying that he would stop drinking. Even the town drunkard signed the pledge and promised to vote for prohibition that day.

The winter of 1883–84 was cruel. In the fall, diphtheria had killed several children and left others in poor shape to fight through until spring.

"All are well," Hulda wrote to her sister, Agnes Miles, in November. "Never better health in my life."

At Christmas the children made their favorite treat to give their friends. First they made small holes at both ends of a raw egg and blew the egg out one end. Then they poured hot maple sugar into the shells and let the eggs cool until the maple sugar hardened. Then they carefully peeled away the shells, revealing perfectly formed eggs of maple sugar candy.

Tad, Bertie, and May had no reason to suspect, in mid-February, that their happy little world was about to fall apart. Hulda went to speak at Springdale meeting, just as she had so many times before. The children went to stay with relatives until she returned.

But their mother collapsed at Springdale, and her friends were afraid she had typhoid fever. They bundled her warmly into a wagon and took her home as fast as they could drive. Hulda Hoover died on First Day morning, February 24, of typhoid and pneumonia. She was only thirty-five years old.

4

Fragments of a Happy Home

"A boy is Nature's answer to false belief that there is no such thing as perpetual motion."

Herbert Hoover

WHAT WAS TO BE DONE about the orphans?

The Hoovers and Minthorns gathered to decide. None could afford to take all three, even though they knew it would have been Hulda's dearest wish to keep them together. Nor did they have any idea how determined the children were to stay together somehow.

At first they remained together—with Grandmother Minthorn and Uncle Merlin Marshall, who had moved to Kingsley in Plymouth County, Iowa. Uncle Merlin's was about as far away from West Branch as one could get and still be in Iowa. Kingsley was on the railroad, two miles from the small town of Oasis. While the boys were there, the townspeople decided to move Oasis—houses, hotel, and town hall—into Kingsley.

"Twenty wagons were under the town hall," said Tad, who probably took Bertie and May to watch the fascinating engineering feat, "hitched together in three rows, and pulled by forty or fifty mules or horses. In just one month, a crop of wheat was growing where the town of Oasis had just been."

In April the Reverend John Y. Hoover, their father's uncle, went out to Kingsley on the train to bring the two boys back to West Branch. The decision had been made.

May, now seven, was to stay with her Grandmother Minthorn in Kingsley. Tad, just turned thirteen, was to live with
his Uncle Henry Davis Hoover in Hardin County, near the
center of the state. He was to work off his board by helping
do the farmwork. When he turned twenty-one, Uncle Davis
promised to give him a team of horses and a wagon so he
could start out on his own as a farmer.

Several people wanted Bertie—the quiet one. His third-
grade teacher, Miss Molly Brown, asked if she could adopt
him. Lawrie Tatum, the family lawyer and a good friend,
decided that an unmarried lady teacher was not what Bertie
needed. Uncle Laban Miles asked to raise him as a brother
to his son Theodore, but Tatum said Indian Territory was no
place to raise a boy. Dr. Minthorn and family had just moved
to Portland, Oregon, and nine-year-old Bertie could not go
out there alone. At last they decided Bertie could live with
Uncle Allen and Aunt Amelia "Millie" Hoover, and so have
Cousin Walter, who was his own age, to walk the mile and
a half to school with.

"Thus were dispersed," Tad wrote sadly, "the fragments of
a happy home."

Almost everything in the House of the Maples was sold.
The children each kept a remembrance. Probably it was May
who kept her mother's case of wax flowers, and Tad who kept
the pair of Texan horns and the hammock. At any rate, it is
certain that Bertie chose for his keepsakes two of his mother's
favorite religious texts, which she had framed and hung on
the wall. One said, "Leave me not; neither forsake me, O
God of my Salvation." The second read, "I will never leave
or forsake thee." The only other items not sold were bedding,
and that was sent with the children to their new homes.

Lawrie Tatum carefully put away the $3,000 that was left
to the children after all the household goods were sold and
debts were paid. This money was for their future education.
He also paid the children's clothing bills and $1.50 a week
for Bertie's board at Uncle Allen's.

Aunt Millie said the boy needed several items of clothing at once: a hat for First Day (fifty-five cents), an everyday hat (fifteen cents), cloth for pants (ninety cents), rubber for garters (seven cents), a scratch book and pencil for school (seven cents), and only two weeks later, another pencil. Bertie had a bad earache (liniment oil, ten cents) that turned out to be caused by an aching tooth (twenty-five cents for pulling tooth).

Aunt Millie was a wonderful cook. The rest of his life Bertie was to compare restaurants and gourmet meals with Aunt Millie's food. She supplied the love and affection he needed as well. Playmates included cousins Alice, fourteen; Walter, ten; Ellen, four; and perhaps the baby Cora. Another baby, Clyde, was not born until four years later.

Uncle Allen's farm, about a mile north of West Branch, had a mortgage. The only money the family spent was for absolute necessities, like paying off the mortgage. Uncle Allen explained carefully to the children what that meant.

"We can't afford to buy anything that we can raise or make. We can butcher our own hogs, make soap and rag rugs, can the fruits and vegetables we raise, gather nuts, and trap rabbits. We make our own clothing and do our own doctoring."

Bertie and Walter helped haul fuel from the woods ten miles away and earned money by picking bugs off the beans (a penny for a hundred) and gathering prickly thistles (nickel a hundred). The latter business picked up considerably in late June, because it was the only way they could afford to buy fireworks for the Fourth of July.

They watched Uncle Allen repair machines that broke down. They tried to build a mowing machine, but it never worked quite right. They had better luck grinding up sorghum grass with an old clothes-wringer, but the molasses syrup they made from it tasted worse than what they used at mealtime for sweetening. Bertie tried not to remember the good taste of sugar that his mother used to buy at the grocery.

"Thee came into this world poor," Aunt Millie told them often, "and worldly things will only corrupt thee."

In that case, Bertie was sure he was in no danger of being corrupted. Aunt Millie wove her own homespun and made everyday clothes for them all.

"My clothes," Bertie said later, "partly homespun and dyed with butternuts, showed no influence of Paris or London."

Meanwhile, Tad never gave up hope of getting the three children back together. He pleaded in vain with Uncle Davis to let Bertie come there to live, promising he would work on the farm until Bertie reached twenty-one.

A constant barrage of letters from one relative to another kept the children in touch somewhat. The family members were still moving farther west. But then came tragic news from Uncle John Minthorn, the doctor who had saved Bertie when he was young. The Minthorn's six-year-old son, Benjamin Bruce, had been killed in a fall from a hay wagon out in Oregon.

"I would like to have Bertie," wrote Dr. Minthorn.

"No boy can fill the shoes of a dead son," said the relatives. "It would be too hard for Bertie."

Doubtless there was also some discussion about Dr. Minthorn himself. He was a very good man, a strong Quaker, but with a personality that not everyone could get along with. He and Laura had moved every few years all their married life. As soon as they arrived in the West he had written back that California was a hideous desert. He had quarreled with the workers in an Indian School in Oregon where he had gone to be the headmaster, and they had moved again.

But Lawrie Tatum, the family adviser whose job it was to support three young orphans until they reached twenty-one, and pay for their education on just $3,000, was not so quick to object. Bertie was a bright boy who could go far with the proper schooling.

Dr. Minthorn was now in Newberg, Oregon, where he was the headmaster of a school called Friends Pacific Academy. The far western state had a healthy climate and offered plenty of opportunities for an alert young man. Besides, where else could Bertie get such a good education free?

The family debated once again. None of them could afford to take Bertie on a week's railroad journey. How could he get there?

A friend from West Branch supplied that answer. Oliver Hammell was taking his family to Oregon from West Branch. Hammell had lost his own son recently from typhoid. Now he wanted to get his family out to the West, where he hoped the air was healthier. They were going by emigrant train—a no-frills ride that would cost Bertie only $27.13. He could travel with them, and Mrs. Hammell would care for him in case he got the croup on the way.

Aunt Millie wiped the tears from her eyes and began sewing a new outfit for Bertie. They had all loved him like their own, but they could not let that blind them to what was best for Bertie. She made and bought him new shirts, a suit of clothes that cost $6.50 and a pair of shoes at $2.25, new pants, boots, overshoes, two pairs of stockings, a fresh box of collars, and two bottles of hive syrup for the croup.

As soon as Tad heard that Bertie was going 2,000 miles away, he hopped on a train to West Branch for a final visit. He found there a tearful Bertie who did not want to leave Uncle Allen, Aunt Millie, and Walter, no matter how exciting it was to see the Pacific Ocean.

Tad had already decided that a farmer's life was not for him, and he knew it was probably not going to suit Bertie either. He had been so hungry for books to read that he had even borrowed a chemistry book from a neighboring teacher.

He sat his brother down for a long talk. Perhaps Bertie would be an inventor, Tad said, like their Grandfather Eli Hoover.

"Just think how famous our grandfather might have been if he had gone to college."

He told Bertie about some of Grandfather Eli's inventions. One was a cattle and hog guard—a gate that allowed the cows to go into the hog yard for a drink of water and wander out

again, without allowing the hogs to leave the yard. And at Uncle Davis's he had seen grandfather's latest invention—a cattle pump.

"A cow steps on a platform and his weight causes the water to be pumped into the trough for a drink! Uncle Davis uses it in a pasture where there is no stream. And don't think cows are dumb! I have seen the same cow get on and off three times to get all the water it wanted."

When Tad promised that some day he would also go to Oregon, Bertie dried his tears and smiled brightly. The big brother could not help admiring the boy. Bertie always managed to find something to be cheerful about—a trait that was not in Tad's nature at all.

5

Emigrants and Zulu Cars

"The boy is a natural spectator. He watches parades, fires, fights, football games, automobiles, and planes with equal fervor. However, he will not watch a clock."

—Herbert Hoover

"GREAT OVERLAND ROUTE," read the Northern Pacific Railroad advertisement in 1885. "Pullman palace sleeping cars, Magnificent day coaches, and Elegant Emigrant sleeping cars with berths free of charge."

The "Elegant Emigrant sleeping cars," according to the ad, were hauled on the rear of the regular trains. But the truth was that the railroad kept their sensitive Pullman travelers as far away as possible from the sight of the poor emigrants. Those who rode the "Elegant Emigrant" cars called them Zulu cars.

On Thursday, November 12, 1885, West Branch people read this item in their weekly newspaper:

"Mr. and Mrs. O. T. Hammell and Bertie Hoover started on their long journey Tuesday evening."

Sometime between November 10, when he boarded the train, and eight days later, when Uncle John Minthorn met him in Oregon, eleven-year-old "Bertie" became Bert Hoover.

In one pocket Bert carried his bottle of hive syrup for the croup. In the other he had a small account book in which he wrote down all the money he had ever had and what he had done with it. The account books, kept by each of the orphans, were probably Lawrie Tatum's idea.

The train boarding was not without tears, handshakes, back pats, many hugs, and promises of letters to be written. All the Hoovers who still lived near West Branch were at the station to say goodbye. Even Mollie Brown, the teacher who had wanted to adopt Bertie, was in the crowd.

Aunt Millie had baked and packed all Bert's favorite foods. He could have fed the entire Hammell family with the fried chicken, ham, bread, meat pies, and other goodies that he carried in a large hamper.

The train rattled across Iowa in a straight line until it reached Council Bluffs, where the travelers met with the emigrant train coming from the crowded eastern cities. Mr. Hammell had spoken the truth when he said the emigrant train was no joyride.

Even though the train was filled with immigrants, most of whom had boarded only a day or so after their boats had landed in America, it was called an "emigrant" train because its passengers would have to "leave" the United States in crossing the country. The Dakotas, Idaho, Utah, and Wyoming were territories, not states. As soon as enough people lived in them to elect representatives and senators, the territories could then become states. California, Oregon, and Washington, even though farther west, were already states.

Greedy land speculators in the East had advertised the cheap train ride heavily and promised the immigrants to America that they could buy cheap land at almost every stop along the way. They had made many more false promises that the poor immigrants were counting on, like free homes, free seeds to plant, free windmills and free wells for drinking water.

Luckily for Bert and the Hammells, some of the passengers thought Council Bluffs was far enough west and got off, leaving a few empty, bare wooden seats. Bert stumbled down the narrow aisle, dragging every item of clothing he owned in a worn leather suitcase that bulged at the corners. The pictured

texts, "Leave me not" and "I will never leave thee," were packed carefully at the bottom, although the frames had had to be left behind for lack of space. On both sides of the aisle, men sprawled across the seats and women tended to numberless dirty-faced children and smelly babies. Everyone wore his oldest clothes for traveling. Bert's own $6.50 suit and $2.25 shoes were carefully packed away until the day he would be dressing for First Day meeting in Newberg, Oregon.

On many emigrant trains, the passengers were crammed ninety to a car. At one end of the car was a kitchen stove for each wife to cook her own family's meals. The wooden seats could be adjusted into bunks at night and so by day were heaped with wobbling towers of blankets and pillows topped with children. Under the seats was baggage, as well as flour sacks filled with bread, vegetables, and other foods for the long trip. The passengers lined up in the morning for a chance to wash their faces in the "convenience," but there was no place to do laundry. The stench of dirty clothes and diapers, blended with the odors of garlic, sauerkraut, salami, cigars, and pipe tobacco, was overpowering.

"At least we don't have to worry about the weather or Indians attacking us," remarked Mrs. Hammell cheerfully, recalling how their ancestors had traveled out to Iowa by covered wagon. Mr. Hammell, who was traveling west for his health, said he was not sure a "Zulu car" was a better way to travel.

Only six years before, Robert Louis Stevenson had traveled across the same route on a train like this. Stevenson was a penniless poet then, hurrying across the United States because the lady he wanted to marry was sick in San Francisco. He described his Zulu car as a "long, narrow wooden box, like a flat-roofed Noah's ark, with a stove and a convenience, one at either end, a passage down the middle, and transverse benches upon either hand." Stevenson took notes and later wrote two books about his trip, *The Amateur Emigrant* and *Across the Plains*.

Most of the passengers on emigrant trains spoke German, Russian, Italian, or a Scandinavian language. Bert had plenty of time for his own thoughts, because he could not understand a word that was said.

Mr. Hammell explained to him that the Northern Pacific Railroad had sent nearly a thousand agents to Europe to encourage large groups of people to emigrate to the land of opportunity. To sell land in the West to them, the railroad advertised with tempting pictures. "California, Cornucopia of the World," read one flyer. "Railroad and Private Land for a Million Farmers . . . a Climate for Health and Wealth without Cyclones or Blizzards."

After the emigrants had signed legal papers they could not understand, many learned that the "free" seed was no good, the "free" windmills and wells did not work, and the "free" homes were not free at all. In about three years, Mr. Hammell predicted, many of the families in their car would lose their life savings. Then, if they wanted to return to the East, they would discover that the low-cost emigrant fares were only for people traveling west!

Bert did not mention whether his train had a "butch" on board, although Stevenson had said it was the butches who gave him the only comforts he had on his trip. A butch was a young boy, usually an orphan, who made his living by selling the passengers fruit, lollipops, cigars, soap, towels, tin washing-dishes, tin coffee pitchers, coffee, tea, sugar, and tinned foods.

A clever butch could make $6,000 in a year, like one butch who passed through a train, selling salted peanuts to everyone. Then, when he was sure the peanuts had made everyone extremely thirsty, he came along selling soda pop. The railroad agents on Bert's train had their own eyes on the emigrants' money, so they may have made certain there would be no butch on this journey.

All day Bert sat by the window and watched the rolling Iowa farmland become treeless Nebraska plains. When the tracks went through towns, he could see the skinny sticks of trees that school children had planted on Arbor Day. This special holiday had begun in Nebraska, where, nine years before, hardly a tree was left in the state.

The train followed the Platte River Valley, just as the wagon trains had. Even now passengers could see families moving west by covered wagon. Sometimes Bert sat with pencil and paper in hand, concentrating hard on Miss Mollie Brown's last assignment—to write her a letter about what he saw from the train window.

There was not a moment of real quiet, day or night. Children wailed, mothers alternately scolded or sang, fathers snored or drank noisily, and someone was always shouting and pointing at a new discovery alongside the tracks.

Every time the train stopped to take on water for the steam boiler, children and even adults hopped off the cars just for the pure pleasure of walking on solid ground and breathing fresh air. The children gathered stones, flowers, sticks, a stray kitten, into their arms for something to play with. But the conductor chased them angrily, shouting, "Get back on the train. Get back." The few of them who did understand him pretended that they did not. Only when the whistle shrieked and the wheels began to turn did they climb back aboard.

One day the conductor went through the train to announce that the Continental Divide was just up ahead. Bert was not sure what to expect at this famous place, where all the waters on the eastern side of the mountains flowed toward the Atlantic and all the waters on the western side flowed into the Pacific. But every important milestone excited the passengers. Two engines were needed now to pull the cars up the mountain slopes. They chugged slower and slower, stopping for more water or fuel and letting off billows of black smoke.

For days he had looked forward to his first sight of the Rocky Mountains, perhaps visualizing some giant rocks like those in Dr. Walker's dental office.

"The Rocky Mountains are disappointing," he wrote Miss Brown. "They are just dirt."

Just east of Ogden, the passengers had to get off the train and change to new cars. For the first time, Bert saw a clean car—although once the passengers settled in they would change the sanitary smell soon enough. At this point, the passengers' names were recorded to show who was going straight west to California, and who would go on to Oregon. The California-bound travelers made jokes about those going to Oregon.

"You'll be growing web feet like all Oregon people, so you can get around in the rain," they joked. Everyone was in good spirits. Only a few more days to go!

The tracks of the Oregon Short Line to Portland headed northwest through Idaho, then along the Columbia River on the Oregon side. The line had been opened only the year before.

Bert had hardly allowed himself to think ahead to that day when the train would arrive in Portland. Now it had to be faced. He was thousands of miles from those he loved and about to become part of a family he hardly knew. His mother used to say, "A way will open up for thee." Then she would say that if the way he had gone was right for him, things would work out. Hadn't things worked out so far? Bert was of too cheerful a nature to worry for long.

He might have been surprised, however, had he known that at that very moment Dr. John Minthorn was also worrying. Minthorn had dearly loved the young son he had buried there in Oregon. And when he asked for his sister's boy to come live with the Minthorn family, he also felt a way had opened up to ease his loneliness.

But Uncle John had always thought Hulda's children were spoiled. She had been far too indulgent, allowing them time for play and giving them no responsibilities and almost no work to do. He owed it to Hulda to make a man of her son. Herbert would be the eldest child in his family. He must be taught to put away childish things now that he was a man of eleven.

When Bert and the Hammells got off the train at Portland station, they breathed the clean air deeply, surprised to find they had become so used to the stink of the car that the fresh air actually smelled unpleasant. The most startling sight caught Bert's eye—a white mountain like a gigantic pyramid. He had seen it from the train, but somehow seeing it in the background of a city, it looked far too large, as if his little sister had drawn it all out of proportion to the trees and houses of the town. For a boy used to the rolling hills of Iowa, Mt. Hood was unbelievable.

Just then Uncle John came toward them. He shook hands solemnly with Mr. Hammell and Bert, and thanked the Hammells for taking his nephew into their care. Bert felt suddenly strange and lonely. He stood silently beside his battered suitcase that now carried the smells and colors of everything that had dropped onto it since they had left Iowa. Uncle John picked it up, hesitated, then tied it onto the rear of his buggy.

Without many more words, Bert and his uncle headed south along the Willamette River toward Newberg. Uncle John was not given to small talk. For better or for worse, Bert was going home.

6

New Family in a New State

"A boy is a piece of skin stretched over an appetite. However, he eats only when he's awake."

—Herbert Hoover

AUNT LAURA could not have known what an impact the sweet smell of bubbling pear butter would have on the nostrils of a growing boy just released from eight days of prison on an emigrant train.

Bert smelled it as soon as he and Uncle John rode into the yard. Aunt Laura and Cousin Tennessee were stirring the huge kettle over an outdoor fire, while the baby, Gertrude, sat watching them. On his way toward the delicious odor, Uncle John told Bert to fetch an armload of wood.

"The meanest thing a man can do is nothing," he said, heaping Bert's arms with logs from a woodpile. "Never allow thyself to have an idle moment."

Bert eagerly helped with the stirring. He had never eaten a pear in his life.

"Eat all thee wants," said Aunt Laura. In the next few hours he made up for the eleven years he had not tasted that fruit, stopping only long enough to gather more wood and stir. Inside him the pears created such a turmoil that it was years before he even tasted another one. Aunt Laura had to dose him with peppermint oil the first night.

The Minthorns' house in Newberg was white frame, with

47

two floors. Bert noticed it had several windows of different sizes and shapes. Aunt Laura's half-sister, Mary Miles, and half-brother, Clark Miles, taught at the school and lived in the house, too.

Bert learned right away that the house was heated by wood, and he was to be the chief log carrier. In Iowa, where wood was rare, houses were heated by coal. But in Oregon, it was just the other way around.

Tennie Minthorn was now ten and very ladylike, not the sort of girl that a boy could take fishing or tramping through the woods. Gertrude was three years old, but she had always been delicate. There would be no romping or roughhousing with her the way he and Tad had brought up their sister, May. Besides, having professors in the house studying all the time was not like being in the midst of Hulda's happy singing or cousin Walter Hoover's noisy games.

Bert dug the bottle of croup medicine out of his coat pocket and set it up on the fireplace mantle.

"I hope I never have to take that stuff again," he remarked. And he never did.

Even before his stomach stopped doing battle with the pears he had eaten, Bert hung his two pictures on the wall of his room. "Leave me not . . ." and "I will never leave thee" hung close together. They gave him a good feeling, as though his mother were talking to him personally.

Dr. Minthorn lost no time introducing Bert to his chores. First the wood needed to be split and carried in. Then Uncle John's matched pinto ponies must be watered, fed, and curried, because a doctor never knew at what hour he might have to hitch up the buggy and ride out into the night. A pony for Tennie and Bert also needed care. The mules, kept to do heavy work, demanded less care than the ponies, but they returned Bert's efforts with a stubbornness that made him dislike them at once. Every morning Bert milked the cows and took them to pasture along Blair Creek. In the afternoon, he drove them back and milked them again. Uncle John could have used Grandpa Eli Hoover's cattle pump, Bert thought, but he would never buy one.

The list of chores seemed endless to Bert. They filled his day from waking to falling asleep. He hated them, and he began very quickly to hate all the animals that stood dumbly waiting for him to attend to their many needs. Not even the offer of a pony of his own could change Bert's feelings. By the time he went to school in the morning, said his friends, he and his clothes smelled just like the barn.

Like many boys, Bert liked to say the best part of school was recess. He endured long hours of study only because when the school days was over, he could run free for a while. Now every minute of free time was taken up with jobs he had to do. Saturdays he did a double load of regular chores, so he would not be guilty of doing work on First Day that could be done at another time. On First Days, Uncle John kept his family busy with Friends' meetings, Sabbath school, prayers, and reading books to improve their souls.

The Friends Pacific Academy schoolhouse sat in the middle of an eighty-acre field, where it had been built the year before. Above the main door was inscribed the motto: WHATSOEVER THY HAND FINDETH TO DO, DO IT WITH THY MIGHT.

Bert could go along with that, but his hand wanted ever so much to go fishing. And he wanted mightily to explore this strange state, where the winter temperature was not even freezing.

Bert and Cousin Tennie were enrolled in the first year of the grammar school where Aunt Laura was principal. Bert thought she must be a warm person deep inside, but her speech was so filled with stern morals that he never found out. After two years of grammar school, the older students had two years of the academy school, with Mr. Starbuck as principal. Then they received a diploma and could go on to college. Uncle John, superintendent of both schools, taught history and literature.

Grammar school cost $7.50 each term, and fifty cents more in the winter, when wood was needed for heat and oil for lamps. But Uncle John paid Bert's tuition. The academy course cost two dollars more. A boarding hall for the girls who came from out of town cost $110 for the whole year, including tuition, food, fire, and lights.

Rules at the school were strict. Newberg was a temperance town, said the catalog, with no saloon nearer than eight miles. A gymnasium was to be built the following year, "so the students will not get their education at the expense of their health and physical vigor." Very few schools had a gym. A gym was usually a barnlike building where the students could do calisthenics, not play games. The new Friends Pacific gym building was to include the boys' dormitory.

"Since immoral and sinful practices are incompatible with the highest mental or physical development," said the catalog, in words that Bert was to hear often from his Uncle John, "no one is desired as a student who will not abstain therefrom. And since some amusements (while they are not considered sinful by some) are calculated to distract the minds of pupils from their studies, they also are strictly excluded from the pastimes or recreations of pupils while attending the academy. (It is) . . . the aim of the instructors to so fill the time with profitable and interesting employment that there will be no room left for evil."

The "profitable and interesting employment" was usually marching, and exercises with Indian clubs. Among the "evil pastimes" was dancing. A pupil who attended a dance was expelled. But Uncle John said if a student made even one little skip while walking, he was "dancing."

"Everything was run with military precision," says Elmer Edson Washburn, a new student at the school in 1886. "Classes marched to study hall and to recitations. At the tap of a small call bell on Dr. Minthorn's desk, we turned in our seats and faced the aisle. At the second tap, we faced either the front of the room as we rose to our feet, or turned to face the rear, according to whether we were going to a recitation seat or to the back of the study hall. At the third tap, we started to the place of recitation. Every move was made quietly and orderly."

Washburn and Bert soon became good friends. Washburn's schooling had been so poor that his family had moved to Newberg just so he could attend the excellent Quaker school. Even though Washburn was sixteen and Bert twelve, they were often in the same classes.

That winter term, Bert learned elocution (the art of speaking in public, gesturing with hands and arms), grammar, geography, and later, composition. He and Washburn were the youngest students in the higher arithmetic classes. They learned arithmetic businessmen needed, like banking, annuities, insurance, partnerships, and building associations. Uncle John had his reasons for wanting Bert to learn about the business world.

School began at nine in the morning with prayers and a twenty-minute talk on a subject intended to build character. One morning the talk was about Joseph and how all the experiences that God allowed him to go through had prepared him to be a good ruler. Uncle John believed that God takes a direct interest in every person and trains that individual for a definite purpose in life. He had not forgotten Grandmother Minthorn's words that morning when he had saved little Bertie's life.

At noon all the students ate dinner in the boarding hall. Afternoon classes were from one until four, and then Bert had to hurry back to the chores again.

The school had a library of carefully selected books, mostly history and biography. None of the "dime novels" that were so popular that year were allowed on the school grounds. Reading "made up" stories was a waste of time, and Dr. Minthorn had a positive genius for making certain that no student had any time to waste. Young people found "relaxing" were soon put to physical labor. Their sweat was needed to help finish the floor, ceilings, and desks on the second floor, and to build the new gymnasium, boarding halls, cottages, woodshed, and barn.

Uncle John was very proud of his school. Such a large school that guaranteed thirty-four weeks of continuous learning was most unusual in a valley filled with pioneers who had barely enough to support themselves. Their wheat crop had failed the year before, and just recently most of the farmers had gone into the fruit and orchard business, planting trees that they hoped would begin to support them in a few years. They were still to discover that even though they grew beautiful fruit, there was not yet a way to get it to market before it spoiled. But their children must have a chance to improve themselves, and so they had built the academy.

Summer brought Bert a release from wood-chopping for the house. But now Uncle John and some of the other men had formed an "improvement company" in Newberg. Bert's latest muscle-builder was helping to cut down tall trees and burn the stumps, to make land ready for building houses. After the trees were cut, he bored a hole about a foot deep straight down through the center of the stump. Then he bored a second hole through the side of the stump, hoping it would meet the first hole. If it missed, he had to bore another. He pushed burning charcoal into the top hole, and blew into the lower hole to start a fire burning.

On a Saturday, he sometimes had a chance to get off into the country and see what Oregon was really like.

"But I was twelve years old," Herbert said when he was older, "before I realized that I might go fishing or camping just for the joy of it, without being struck down by an angry Lord for not being faithful."

When he did go exploring, he did not go on horseback. Bert and the pony that was to be his were never friends.

One day Uncle John had to send medicine to a patient who lived far out in the country. He sent for Bert and handed him the package.

"Take the horse," the doctor insisted.

But Bert was determined. No horse. He would rather walk the whole way. Dr. Minthorn was just as determined and getting angrier every minute. He led Bert out to the barn, saddled up the horse himself, and sat Bert on it.

"Thee must learn to ride a horse," he demanded. "Now get thee out and learn."

Uncle John never knew how long Bert stayed on the horse that he rode out of the barnyard that day, but when Herbert returned, he was on foot, leading the horse. He tried only one more time.

Coming home from a camping trip in the mountains, Bert had to drive a span of mules back with an empty wagon. He started down a very steep hill. Suddenly the rear wagon wheels began to slide in the mud. The wagon skewed around and the bed of the wagon came apart. Bert was thrown off into the bushes. The rear wheels went in another direction, and the terrified mules ran on down the hill, pulling the front wheels and a part of the wagon with them. No amount of persuasion from Uncle John could get Bert to trust a mule or horse again.

That summer, Herbert worked for Alva Cook, who lived about six miles from Newberg on "beaverdam" land. When Alva needed more help, Bert suggested his friend Washburn. The two boys worked on their knees, straddling onion plants and pulling up the weeds. They worked twelve hours a day for two weeks. At night they collapsed onto a mattress made of oat straw on the attic floor of Cook's cabin. The rest of the summer, Bert worked in Hoskin's brickyard back in Newberg. Bert much preferred such back-breaking work to caring for Uncle John's animals.

In midsummer Bert went on a camping trip with the family and some friends. One person had volunteered to be the cook, but said he would do it only until someone complained about the food. At that moment, the faultfinder was to become the cook. When dinner was served the first night, some hemlock needles had fallen onto the potatoes.

"Needles in the potatoes . . . ?" began a voice. The cook turned around quickly to see who had just volunteered for his job.

"Oh, I *like* them this way," Bert finished quickly.

That night the temperature plunged downward, and the campers found they had not brought enough blankets. They had no warm sleeping bags, and the chilly air kept them tossing all night, trying to get warm. In the morning, Dr. Minthorn asked Bert how he had slept.

"Often," was the reply.

Late in the summer of 1886, Elmer Washburn was hired to do the job Bert hated most—caring for the horses. Bert still was on hand, however, to hitch up the pintos when the doctor was called out in the night. On the long rides with his uncle, Bert learned a great deal about medicine, the Battle of Shiloh, sick people, the Civil War, and the Oregon countryside. Uncle John was a born teacher, and those midnight rides could be put to a useful purpose just as well as the schoolroom.

Herbert spent as much time as he could at Washburn's house. Mrs. Washburn often sewed on missing buttons and enjoyed watching him wolf down her good cooking. He was neglected in many ways, she told her husband. And it was clear that Bert was not happy. Uncle John said Bert resented being told to do his chores. Aunt Laura said she was tired of always saying, "It's time for thee to bring in the wood."

Bert probably wrote letters to his brother about his unhappiness, but no complaining letters survive. As he grew older, Bert outgrew his rebellious feelings. Meantime, there was only anger and misunderstanding between the boy and his elders.

One day late in September of 1887, Bert came running to Washburn's house. His round, pink cheeks were flushed with excitement. His brother Tad was coming to Oregon.

"I want you to be the first one to meet Taddie," he told his friend, "and I want you to like him."

The Minthorn household had now added a new baby, Mary Agnes, so there was no room in the house for Tad. Uncle John said he would fix a room in the academy building where Bert and Tad could live. They could eat their meals with the family.

Tad had reached sixteen, and it was obvious to both him and Uncle Davis Hoover that he would never become a farmer. His uncle released him from their agreement, and Lawrie Tatum gave him enough of his inheritance money to buy a ticket to Portland, Oregon.

Tad took a regular train. The emigrant train took at least two days longer to travel, because it was constantly being shunted off on sidings to let the regular trains go through. With twenty dollars in his pocket, Tad reached Council Bluffs at night. He curled up in an empty chair car to wait for his overland train. It was Tad's last good sleep for six days. He arrived in Portland on Saturday afternoon. No train went to Newberg until the next Monday afternoon. His impatience to see Bert had been building for two years. He could not wait another day. He bought a ticket for his trunk to ride from Portland to Newberg, and started to walk the forty miles.

But walking in Oregon was not like taking a hike in Iowa.

First there was Portland, the largest town Tad had ever seen. Soon after he passed the last house, the road plunged into a heavy forest where the trees were two and three hundred feet tall. Tad had never even imagined such a forest. No birds were singing. Or were they? He could not tell. If there were any birds they were so high up, where the sun touched the treetops, that no human ear could hear them. A carpet of pine needles softened his footsteps and made the silence even more frightening.

It was worse after sunset. Even when there was not a single star shining, the prairies were never so dark as the forest in Oregon that night. He could not see the path. And because of the pine needles, his feet could not feel the edge of the path.

Suddenly a horse and rider came up behind him. He hardly had time for fear before he heard a friendly "halloo." The westerner lived in the next town and offered Tad a bed for the night. The next day the stranger hitched up his wagon and drove Tad the rest of the way to Newberg.

Bert invited Washburn to come to his new room to meet Tad. But although they were the same age, Tad and Washburn did not click. Tad had smuggled onto the school grounds a Bill Nye joke book called *Baled Hay*. He insisted on reading aloud the best parts. Washburn was not impressed. But Bert did not give up easily. He managed it so that the three of them were together so often that the boys wound up best friends after all. Bert's next project was to get Tad to stay in Oregon.

"Thee must go to school—first, last and always," Dr. Minthorn told Tad. But he would have to earn the money to pay for it. The next day Tad began cutting cordwood. At the end of a ten-hour day, he proudly held two dollars to start paying his tuition. Tad entered the school in the same class with Bert.

In their small sleeping room, Bert often lay awake for hours with an earache. And then there were the uninvited occupants of the room. The first few mornings, Tad's legs were covered with sores from scratching the fleabites while he was asleep. Bert suggested that he tie his hands. He did, and the sores went away, but the fleas did not. Only when they scrubbed the floor with kerosene once a week were they able to limit the flea population.

Herbert fell in love that winter. Daisy Trueblood was in the second year of grammar school, and Bert had advanced to the first year in the Academic Department. He had not yet begun to grow tall, so Daisy's eyes often looked right past Bert toward his older brother. After many erasings and ink-blots, Bert finally wrote her a letter.

> *Friend Daisy,*
>
> *(and I hope you are more than my friend, although I do not dare to head it that way yet) You do not know the extent to which I am enthralled, and I am sure that no girl should be allowed such mastery over any person's heart, unless there are such feelings in her own heart. I could not have helped paying my attentions to you, if I had tried and I am sure I did not try very hard. I do not think you care. Do you?*
>
> *Answer this please*
>
> *Bert*

But the restless Dr. Minthorn was about to move his family again, this time to Salem, about twenty-five miles away by river. Bert packed his few clothes, the pictures from his mother, and his memories of Daisy Trueblood.

Uncle John offered to pay him fifteen dollars a month to work in the Salem office of a new business he was starting. At fourteen, he was still too young to go to college. And the idea of making real money, instead of pennies, sounded good to Herbert.

7

Salem Wheels and Deals

*"I am sure I'd have made a better all-around man if I hadn't lost
so much time just making a living."*

—Herbert Hoover

DURING THE SUMMER of 1888, Tad and Bert helped the Minthorns move to Salem, Oregon. They took the cows and horses
overland. Then they hauled the rest of the movables down
to the steamboat landing on the Willamette River and sent
them by boat to Salem.

Dr. Minthorn had joined several other Quakers, including
Ben Cook, Fred Cottle, and Charles Moore, in a land settle-
ment business. They bought land cheaply in Salem and sold
it to the new settlers who were beginning to flock to the West
Coast. They bought thousands of trees and planted fruit orchards, so the land would be more valuable.

Uncle John built his barn first, in an area he called "the
Highland Addition," north of Salem. Since only the barn was
finished when Aunt Laura arrived with Tennie, Gertrude,
baby Mary Agnes, Bert, and the furniture, they all lived in
it until the house was finished.

Next door, Uncle John began building another house so
that Grandmother Minthorn and Tad and Bert's sister, May
Hoover, could move there from Iowa. At last, Hulda and
Jesse's children would be almost together again.

Tad worked at the sawmill west of Newberg to save money

59

for his education. He did not want to move to Salem with Bert and the Minthorns. Tad and Uncle John needed much space between them.

Herbert Hoover stopped in his tracks and stared into the window of the cycle shop. What he saw was no ordinary bicycle. The bikes the local wheelmen used had one giant wheel with a small wheel behind. He had seen their hapless riders tumbling off and taking a header into the bushes whenever their high wheels hit a pebble or pothole. On a downhill run they risked their lives, because their cycles had no brakes.

The object of beauty that struck Bert dead in his tracks had two wheels of the same size. The rider sat on a small saddle, not high off the ground as he would on a horse, but close enough for his feet to touch the ground. It even had a brake. The rider of a safety bicycle such as this would not have to go downhill at breakneck speed or aim for a soft bush to land in when a child ran across his path or a dog tried to bite his wheels.

Herbert's account book, always in his pocket, allowed no money for extravagances. Bert was a business man now that he had stopped school for a while. The Victor "Safety Bicycle," made by Overman in San Francisco, was cheaper than a horse, and it did not need to be curried, fed, or stabled. But it still cost almost a hundred dollars. The longer he gazed at the shiny bicycle, the more he wanted to possess it.

Dr. Minthorn surprised him by agreeing. For a boy who would not get on a horse or even behind one in a buggy, the Victor was not a bad idea, said his uncle. He loaned Bert the extra money, taking a little out of his pay each month.

Roads were either muddy or dusty, depending on the weather. None were paved. But the hardest part of being a bicycle rider was resentment from the rest of the traffic. Farmers drove their wagons in the middle of the road and got fiercely angry when a bicyclist wanted to pass. Coach drivers, who had more sensitive horses than farmers, waved their whips dangerously close and accused Bert of frightening their horses by coming up from behind. Children thought it great sport to run into the road and try to catch sticks in the wheel spokes.

One day Tad and Bert went on a fishing trip to the Santiam. Bert had no trouble finding perfect fishing worms in the plowed land of the new development. But the fish did not even nibble at their hooks. Other fishermen passed them with long strings of fish they had caught. Tad suggested they try using some of the tough bread that Bert had made himself and brought for their lunch. The fish ignored that, too. At last one of the fishermen took pity on the boys.

"That's not the way to catch fish," he said.

He showed them how he used a "fly" made of colored feathers and how he tossed his fishing line so it landed exactly where he wanted it to drop in the water.

"It has to drop without making a splash or a sound," he told Bert. "Fish are not stupid, you know."

The Hoover boys had never heard of fishing without worms. The experienced fisherman gave each of the boys two trout flies to keep.

All afternoon they fished with their new flies. Bert and Tad never noticed that it had grown quieter. Suddenly they realized the sun was setting and that it had been several hours since other fishermen has passed by.

Darkness fell with the suddenness of pulling down a window shade. Before they could gather their belongings, the trail had become too dark to find their way home. Even though Bert had his Victor and Tad his second-hand bicycle, the dirt road was impossible to travel in the inky black night.

They ate fish for dinner, and even Bert's homemade bread suddenly seemed more tasty. They saved some of the bread for morning and fell asleep under a bush. But breakfast time never came, because something stole their bread while they slept.

"Never mind," Bert told Tad. "Whatever ate my bread will not live to get far, and then we can eat it."

That summer, Herbert fell in love with fishing. He used

the flies that the fisherman had given to him until not a feather was left on them to lure a fish to the frying pan. Forever after, when Herbert Hoover wanted to relax and get away from the cares of the world, he took his bait box and fishing pole and headed for the woods.

In Salem, whenever friends or relations invited him along on a camping trip, Bert got out his bicycle. Dr. Minthorn always asked if he did not want to ride with them in the buggy.

"I'll be there waiting when thee comes," said Bert. And he was, even though the trip might be twenty-five miles and uphill all the way.

Every day Bert rode his cycle from Highland Addition into Salem to open the office. Hardly a minute of his day was dull. Bert kept track of all the office work and papers of the Oregon Land Company and took on many "extras" besides. The land company had built a church, for example, but there was no congregation, yet, to sit on its benches. Bert's job included arranging for a preacher to come and recruit new church members for the empty building. Sixty members joined the church the next Sunday.

Near the church, the land company built houses, a hotel, and a schoolhouse. The Oregon Land Company also owned and ran a sawmill and flour mill. Businesses moved in, including one that would dry the fruit that the new residents were going to grow in their orchards. The company graded the streets and built a water system.

Uncle John Minthorn was president of the Oregon Land Company. The men who had formed the company had so many projects going at once that they had little time to sit in the office. They called Bert their "walking encyclopedia," because he knew everything that was going on. Even Uncle John was amazed at what good business sense his nephew had. Before too long, Herbert was making twenty dollars a month— a fortune to the boy who had once picked a hundred thistles for a nickel.

Bert rarely had any spare time. When he did, he put it to good use. Once he and a friend went into the sewing machine business together. They bought twenty dollars worth of broken sewing machines and put them together again. But customers refused to buy them, even though they cost only one dollar. Bert had better success talking the office bookkeeper into teaching him how to keep financial records. Then he talked Miss Laura Heulat, the office secretary, into teaching him how to type.

Herbert enjoyed advertising the properties the Oregon Land Company had to sell, because he loved the Oregon countryside. "No Hot Night in Summer—Grass Grows All Winter" blared one newspaper ad that also informed readers that Oregon had "no cyclones, blizzards, grasshoppers." The ads appeared in over a thousand Midwest and eastern newspapers. People who had decided to move west began arriving in Salem from all parts of the country.

When the newcomers wrote ahead, Herbert met them at

the railroad station. A great many competing land companies also sent their office boys to the railroad to look for likely buyers and drag them to their own offices. For such an occasion, Bert agreed to use Uncle John's pintos and the buggy, whisking his own customers safely away from the competition. He showed them the houses the Oregon Land Company had to rent or sell, pointing proudly to the school, church, and hotel already built.

By the time the circus came to Salem in June of 1889, Bert could also point out the Salem Street Railway that his company was building. Personally, Bert would have liked the railway better if the cars were not pulled by horses. But there were fringe benefits. Between the two steel rails, good fir planks had been laid for the horses to walk on. These made a smooth and safe place for Bert to ride his Victor bicycle all the way from home to the office.

The Grand Olympian Festival arrived in Salem with a noisy, but free, street parade to show Salem's citizens what was meant by "intellectual and refined amusement," as advertised in the newspaper. The Sells brothers claimed to have brought to Oregon not only the two biggest shows on earth, but "the absolute and only Eureka of Canvas entertainments."

Gymnasts and aerialists paraded beside wrestlers and boxers. Gladiators flanked the wheeled lion cages, waving their swords as if they were there to protect the crowds in case one of the dangerous beasts should escape. Romans in gold and white costumes rumbled past Bert's office in golden painted chariots. Elephants, a camel, tigers, and ladies who stood on the backs of prancing horses all made Salem people hungry to see the circus and the "bewildering and inexplicable Meteoric Surprises" promised after dark. These turned out to be fireworks.

Every September the Oregon State Fair was held at Salem. For this special event, Herbert Hoover was in charge of planning how many extra cars, horses, drivers, and conductors the Salem Street Railway needed to carry the crowds of people one mile out of town to the fairgrounds.

Bert had only one worry. Tad had hopped from one job to another all summer. None suited him. Just before school started, he had wildly hopped a freight train and gone off to see what the rest of Oregon looked like. When Tad returned to school in Newberg again, he was more rebellious than ever. The stiff rules at Friends Pacific Academy had been made for babies, Tad said. And he had had all the forced labor he could stand. He was going on nineteen and wanted to go to a dance or go fishing on the Sabbath or read joke books, if he so desired. One night Tad was seen at a dance. The next day he quit school before they could expel him. He was free at last.

Bert missed going to school so much that he had enrolled in a free night school, where he studied mathematics and Latin. He was unusually good at higher math, but Latin was much harder than he expected.

One day when Herbert was struggling with Latin during a lull in the office, a lady stopped at his desk with a cheerful "hello." Miss Jane Gray, daughter of a bank president, had taken on a special job. Salem was filled with nice young men who had had to leave school and work for their living. Most of them had never had a chance to sample the finer things in life.

"I teach a Sunday School class at the Presbyterian church for boys like you who have to work," she told Bert pleasantly. "Will you come to the class and then to our home for dinner afterwards?"

Bert never passed up a good meal. And he was lonely. Working all day, sometimes until ten at night, he had no chance to meet many boys his own age. Miss Gray left a library book for Bert to read.

He looked down at the book after she left. It was called *Ivanhoe* and was certainly not the sort of book Uncle John would allow him to read. He opened it, curious to see what a forbidden "made-up" story looked like. A few minutes later the office boy had lost himself in a world of knights and maidens in distress. Perhaps Tad was not the only rebel in the family after all.

Miss Gray was a good judge of character. Of the four boys that Bert met in Miss Gray's Sunday School class the next Sunday, one later became a famous doctor in New York, one a law professor at Stanford, and one, Burt Brown Barker, became Bert Hoover's best friend. The fourth died while still a young man.

But right now the class had five gawky boys in it. All of them had legs about six inches too long for the trousers they were wearing. They had no idea how to meet a nice girl who would invite them to a party, or how to behave at a party in case one did. Bert had never even seen powdered sugar until that Sunday dinner at the Grays'. Miss Gray talked of an endless list of good books the boys might like to read—*The Last of the Mohicans, David Copperfield,* and others. Bert's small world began to expand.

Uncle John, and even the Hoover relatives, thought art, music, and the theater were a waste of time. And wasting time was evil. Grandmother Minthorn knew what temptation was. Even though she wore only somber gray and black Quaker dress, in her heart she loved bright colors. Hidden in her wedding chest were gaily colored designs for quilts that she had never stitched because they were entirely too cheerful for a Quaker household. Bert decided his strict relations were happier not knowing about the new world he was discovering. Many nights after work he slept in the back room at the office.

The office was usually open until 10:00 P.M., sometimes for business and sometimes because the company's owners sat around discussing politics. One of the owners was Oregon's superintendent of public instruction, and the company cashier was the Speaker of the state's lower house. Herbert learned a great deal about local government and world affairs from these men. He decided that politics was not a very high calling, but public service was.

One night, the men were particularly noisy. They had argued long and hard, and Bert could see they were never going to agree. Suddenly the gas lights flickered and went off. The men decided it was time to go home anyway.

"Bert, did thee turn out the lights?" Uncle John asked with a twinkle in his eye when they were closing the door.

Bert grinned a little. "They were only running up the gas bill," he admitted. "There was no use in that kind of talk."

Uncle John's quiet chuckle sounded good to Bert. Things had not been going well in business for Dr. Minthorn lately, and Tad had added greatly to his worries. Tad had left his job on Salem's daily newspaper and was going to work in a brewery.

"Thee will fill a drunkard's grave!" Uncle John had roared at Tad so loudly that Bert was sure people outside could hear. "And thee missed meeting again last First Day."

Tad tried to explain that a camping trip along the coast on First Day had given him much more uplift than going to meeting. As for the brewery, he was trying to earn money to go to college.

"How much money has thee saved?" Uncle John demanded angrily. He calmed down when Tad showed him his account book. He had saved enough for half of a four-year course.

"If I pay for the other half, will thee go this fall term to Penn College?" he asked. Tad had agreed, and he had left for the college in Oskaloosa, Iowa.

Bert smiled as he read Tad's letter. At roll call in chapel the first day, the new students' names had been called out. The fourth student was Millie Branson, the fair, brown-eyed girl he had worshipped across the wooden divider at West Branch meetinghouse. When he had looked at the grown-up Millie, and she saw his freckles were gone, Tad had a feeling that he would never have to be alone again.

Bert Hoover's whole life was about to change, too, when a young engineer, Robert Brown, came into the office. While Bert was growing up, the term "engineer" was used for almost any man who could drive a train, put a sewing machine together, or dig in a coal mine. Today, Brown told Bert, engineering was a profession like being a doctor or lawyer. For ten years, the United States Geological Survey had been mapping the location of mineral deposits for the Department of the Interior. Its geologists had learned their profession in an engineering college.

Herbert Hoover had never forgotten his beloved rock collections. One was still in Uncle Laban's attic in Pawhuska. A geologist had plenty of chance to live outdoors. Camping and even fishing fit in well with a geologist's way of life. Bert began sending for information from colleges where he could learn about geology.

Grandmother Minthorn had some choice words to say when Bert announced that he had chosen his college. She had hoped he would choose a Quaker school where he might get a scholarship. At least he might have chosen an old, established school with some ivy growing up the walls.

But Bert reminded her how many times the way had opened up for him to go to a *new* school, or live in a *new* town, or work in a *new* business. Now he was going to a *new* university to study a *new* science.

He did not mention that the way had not actually opened up for him. The Stanford catalog listed many requirements that he could not meet. He would have to study harder than ever, and even then, he might have to batter the door down to get in.

8

Home at Last in Stanford

"If it were not for boys, the newspapers would go undelivered and unread and a hundred thousand picture shows would go bankrupt."
—Herbert Hoover

BERT'S HEART SANK every time he read through the list of subjects he had to know before he could get into Stanford. He had learned the arithmetic that a businessman needed, but he knew nothing of algebra, geometry, and something even harder, called trigonometry. He had never studied Greek, and he had just started Latin in the night school. He had never learned a modern foreign language or studied any science in a laboratory such as biology, chemistry, or physics.

"I suppose I know English well enough?" he asked Miss Gray hopefully. But she told him the college would expect him to be able to write good compositions with perfect spelling and punctuation, discuss plays by Mr. William Shakespeare, and perhaps quote some lines from famous poems. Bert's faint hopes sank once again.

Miss Gray said Bert had not even learned much about what was happening outside of his own little world in Salem. Uncle Laban had told him the year before about the Oklahoma land rush. Twenty thousand people had ridden at breakneck speed across his state, knocking each other out of the way, in order to grab for themselves land that had been promised to the Indians. In another section of the country, Americans were now building their homes on land given by treaty to the Sioux Indians. Chief Sitting Bull had been killed in South Dakota.

New York City now had a skyscraper with a steel skeleton, eleven stories tall, and another skyscraper was going up in St. Louis. Chicago had the tallest building in the U.S., twenty stories high. Bert and Miss Gray tried to count the exciting inventions of just the past few years—incandescent light bulbs, telephones in some city homes, a phonograph machine, cushion tires for Bert's bicycle, a machine that sewed by electricity, an electric chair that had been used for the first time to electrocute a criminal, and a "Kodak" camera so simple that even a child could now take a photograph. Thomas Edison had just patented a camera that he claimed could take moving pictures. Another inventor had just patented a hookless fastener that was to change the clothing industry. Later it was known as the "zipper."

When Herbert had the deepest doubts about being admitted to the only college where he wanted to go, he remembered that he still had one thing going for him. He knew how to work hard.

In the summer of 1891, Bert went to Portland to take entrance examinations to see whether he could qualify for Stanford. Fred Williams, son of a Salem banker, went with him. The boys passed everything until the exam on mathematics. Professor Joseph Swain, a Quaker, was in charge of that important test. Fred knew no more math than Bert, because Bert had been tutoring him. The boys sat on the edge of their seats.

"I saw Bert Hoover put his teeth together with great decision," Swain said later. "His whole face and posture showed his determination to pass the exam."

But too many of the problems were beyond Bert. As the hours wore on, he sank lower in his seat. At last he had to turn in his paper, half-finished.

"Have any trouble?" Swain asked kindly. The professor learned that Bert had studied his way through the first two geometry books, but some of the problems he had tried to solve were based on the fourth book. Swain asked the two boys to come to his room at the hotel.

"He came promptly," Swain said. The more he talked with Fred and Bert, the more determined Swain became that the university needed those boys as much as the boys needed it.

"Hoover was without money, but ready to do anything he could to make his way and get a college education. Such a boy only needs to be given a chance," Swain told President David Starr Jordan later.

At last, Hoover and Williams were told they could arrive three months early on the campus. They were to board at Adelante Villa and be tutored in math and English by two schoolteachers, Lucy Fletcher and Eleanor Pearson. The boys would have to take another exam in September.

News came from Lawrie Tatum, back in Iowa, that Bert's share of the "education money" left by his parents came to $822.67. Somehow that money had to stretch over four years. Bert knew he would have to sell his bicycle and work his way through college.

Before he left Oregon, Bert went on his Victor bicycle to say goodbye to his old friends in Newberg. He tried to talk Elmer Edson Washburn into going to Stanford with him, but Washburn had saved only about $200.

"So he tried to sell me his bicycle, but I could not afford that either," said Washburn, many years later. "I have often wondered just what course my life would have taken if I had gone to Stanford with him."

Herbert sold his bicycle and everything else he could part with. He was almost seventeen when he and Fred Williams took the train to California. They walked from the station in Menlo Park up the dusty, unpaved road to the ranch land where the new college buildings were going up.

"Where is Adelante Villa?" they asked some workmen. The men pointed to a plain farmhouse, now coated with dust. All the hot summer they lived there, studying English, geography, mathematics, and American history. Bert paid for his board and lessons by caring for the ladies' horses.

Only a day before the important exams, Hoover discovered he would be tested in one of the sciences. He looked at the list, fighting down the panic inside. Physiology? That was the stuff his Uncle John had talked to him about on all those midnight rides to visit patients. He sat up all night reading two textbooks on physiology. By morning he was ready.

Bert passed everything but the dreaded English composition exam. He passed it only "on condition." He could enter Leland Stanford Junior University, but sometime before his graduation four years away he must pass the English exam.

The university was named for Leland Stanford, Jr., who had died of typhoid before he was sixteen. His father, Leland Stanford, had been governor of California and president of the Central Pacific Railroad, and was just starting his career as a U.S. senator when the crushing blow came. All his money had not been able to save his son.

Being wealthy, Stanford could build a magnificent tomb for his boy, but the designs that architects dreamed up gave him no comfort. Then one sleepless night, he began to dream of a new kind of university in California. In a way, all its students would become his children. Tuition was to be free, and Senator Stanford wanted the cost of board to be as cheap as possible, so even a poor boy could afford to work his way through. His new college was to hire young teachers with new ideas, but who were top men in their fields.

The new university was built on land that had been Stanford's ranch in the Santa Clara Valley, thirty miles south of San Francisco. It was not ready to open until October 1, 1891.

The first president of the university, David Starr Jordan, was a New York farm boy who hated farming. He had become a famous naturalist, a mountain climber, and a founder of the

Sierra Club, and had campaigned for Mount Rainier and Yosemite to become national parks.

Now, in 1891, Jordan's notebook was filled with his ideas for the new college. Books were important, but unless students went out into the field they could never understand nature. Field trips were a new idea in education in those days. Jordan filled his pocket notebook with names of teachers his friends had suggested he hire for the new university. As he met each one, he made a notation beside the name.

"A peculiarly strong man in biological research, also of very attractive personality," he wrote after one name. And beside another, he wrote, "Won't do—is erratic," and "too narrow—ambitious chiefly to be called to Harvard".

One of the first professors Jordan invited to the new college was Dr. John Caspar Branner, who was then head of the Natural History Department at Indiana University. Branner always took his botany and geology students on "foot excursions." Bert had heard that Branner was the best geology professor anywhere. He would have gone to the ends of the earth just to study with him.

Herbert Hoover and Fred Williams were the first students to move into the men's dormitory, Encina Hall. The other students began arriving in a week. When the dining hall opened, Bert could hardly believe his eyes. For as far back as he could remember, his breakfasts had always been the same tasteless items.

"The dining room gave so many options in food," he wrote his brother, "that I was able to declare my complete independence from mush and milk!"

Life changed quickly when the other dormitory students arrived. They came loaded down with possessions that transformed each bare room into what Bert thought looked more like the throne room for a rajah. Boys puffed up the stairs carrying lace curtains and tapestry bedspreads, oriental rugs, velvet chairs that lay back, potted plants, bookcases, family photographs, bear rugs, tiger rugs, brass candy dishes, leather cushions, and antlers. What all this had to do with getting a college education, Herbert was soon to learn.

The "frats" came around to visit the first week. They looked over Bert and his room, furnished with only the bare necessities and none of the signs that marked it as "civilized."

"We plan to have fraternities here at Stanford," one boy said impressively. When Bert did not look impressed, he went on, "Any man who does not join a fraternity will automatically become a 'barb.' "

Bert said nothing. Silence was his usual response to a strange situation, but the "frats" had no way of knowing that.

"A barbarian, of course," said another "frat," in a voice that showed a barb was at the lowest depth of the social scale.

Fraternities cost money, so Bert immediately became a barb. Soon the frats elected their own members to all the student offices. The barbs complained that the officers had a very loose way of handling the money of the student organizations, and said they would like to see some accounting.

Herbert's job in the university office at five dollars a week gave him money to eat. He started a newspaper route and, when he discovered the students had no way to clean their clothes, began a laundry service. He picked up a student's dirty clothes, delivered them to the laundry, and returned them to the closet again. He bought a dilapidated old bicycle, tore it apart, and fixed it up for transportation. Soon business was so good that he hired other students to help.

Hoover played shortstop on the baseball team. But after only a few games the other players convinced him he would be a much better manager. His job would be to arrange games, raise money to buy uniforms and equipment, and collect money at the gate, although, so far, the playing field had neither fence nor gate. Townspeople flocked across an open field to see Stanford play baseball. Hoover's job was to collect twenty-five cents from each.

"We usually let him go in free," a helper told him one day, pointing to a man who Bert thought looked as if he could well afford the quarter. He was so outraged that he gave chase and collected one dollar, for which he gave the man four tickets. Bert's helper collapsed in laughter.

"That's Mr. Benjamin Harrison," he told Bert. "Former President of the United States."

One time, when the team played in Santa Rosa, only a few people went to the game, and so the players did not have enough money to get back to school. Hoover had to ask for money from some of the students' parents who lived in the town.

"Some of them were very caustic persons," he said dryly, as he bought the team's railroad tickets that night.

Hoover entered Stanford as a mechanical engineering major. Dr. Branner did not arrive at Stanford until the start of the second semester, so it was January before Bert could study geology. As soon as Branner discovered Hoover could typewrite, he gave him a job as his office assistant.

At twenty dollars a month, Encina Hall was too expensive for Hoover. He saw the other boys in the dormitory spend more money in a weekend than he had seen in his life. It was depressing. When the price increased the next year, he and some friends moved into a boardinghouse nearby, called Romero Hall. By then his inheritance was down to $418.17.

The first summer, Dr. Branner got Herbert Hoover a job as an assistant doing a geological survey of Arkansas. The job paid sixty dollars a month—a fortune to Bert. But it was no easy desk job. He walked hundreds of miles, measuring and mapping fourteen townships in three counties in the Ozarks.

The mountain people were highly suspicious of the strange, quiet boy. Was he looking for moonshiners? Revenue agents usually talked a lot more. They wondered why he was measuring the land, unless he planned to build a factory. When they saw him looking at rocks and following veins of coal, they thought he might be hunting for gold. At first, Hoover had tried to explain he was a geologist, but in the end it was easier not to explain.

At night he asked the mountain people in the nearest cabin for a place to sleep. The people shared their sorghum molasses, cornmeal, and sowbelly dinners with him, but they did not trust him. During that summer, Hoover was on the edge of Osage country. He located vast limestone deposits and named them Pawhuska Limestone for Uncle Laban's favorite Indian.

The day before school opened, Herbert wrote a letter to a friend back in Salem. He promised to send him a catalog of Stanford. But even the fortune earned surveying was not going to make his second year at Stanford easy.

"Am going into the baggage business at the beginning of school," he wrote. "Got the encouraging news from my guardian that he has not a cent, and consequently am out with just $46.23 to get through the year. Dr. Branner says I can swim it. If not, he will throw in a cork . . . Have considerable business worked up and 30000000000 schemes for making more. May the gods use you better than I . . ."

Hoover was sure now that he wanted to be a geologist. He moved back into the dormitory because the college campus had become his home. He signed up for the hardest courses he could find. The "condition" in English still had to be taken care of, but it seemed a waste of money to pay for a course in something he could learn by himself—whenever he had the time.

He saved so much of the school's money from baseball that Stanford could now afford a football team. They made Hoover manager of that, too. When he had 10,000 tickets printed for a Thanksgiving football game against the University of California, Herbert remembered that embarrassing evening in Santa Rosa. But this time a huge audience showed up. Twenty thousand of them. But Herbert had no time to worry about how they were to fit into 15,000 seats.

The field was now fenced in, but the ticket collectors at the gate had a fast-growing problem. California still did not use much paper money. Most people paid for their tickets in silver and gold. Bert had to run to some houses nearby and borrow dishpans and washboilers to hold all the money.

In the midst of the coin clanking, the team captains came running over to him. Where was a football? Nobody had brought one. The game was delayed while Bert sent a boy into town to buy two pigskins.

All night, Bert and the manager for the other team sat up counting the money. Next morning they carried washtubs to the bank with $30,018.

The World's Columbian Exposition in Chicago the summer of 1893 was to be the most elegant world's fair the United States ever held. About February, Bert began helping Dr. Branner build a huge relief map of Arkansas, weighing well over a ton, to show at the fair.

The rest of the summer Herbert spent in Oregon collecting fossils for Dr. Branner and visiting his brother. Tad had left Penn College and was working in the printing business. Herbert probably visited the Minthorns too. Cousin Tennie was studying music at Willamette University, but in 1892 she died of a flu virus at age seventeen. Chubby Bert had become tall, thin, and scholarly looking now that he had to wear glasses. A case of measles had damaged his eyesight the first year at college.

With two more years of college still ahead, Herbert Hoover's money had now dwindled down to $110.26. He carried a very heavy course load and, as usual, had no time to pass the English exam that was still hanging over him. The battle between the "frats" and the "barbs" came to a head. No one seemed to be watching over the student body's money. The Glee Club ran up huge bills. The athletic team managers kept no account of the gate receipts. The barbs decided to put an end to the frats' poor business skill. They roused the students to vote for a constitution. Then came the election. Herbert Hoover became student body treasurer. His friend Lester Hinsdale became president, and another friend, Herbert Hicks, became football manager.

By the end of his junior year, Herbert's education fund was down to $12.74. A well-paying summer job in 1893 was more important than ever. Dr. Branner found Bert a job with the team doing the geological survey of California and Nevada. Dr. Waldemar Lindgren, one of the best geologists in the U.S., was to be his chief. But when summer came, the job still looked indefinite.

Hoover's friends talked him into going with them to Yosemite. All along the way, they painted advertising signs for a San Francisco newspaper to pay for their trip. Almost as soon as he reached Yosemite, Hoover received a telegram telling him to be in the Sierra Mountains to meet Dr. Lindgren within a few days. All the boys together did not have enough money to pay for Bert's train fare to Stockton, where he was to board a riverboat. So he walked the eighty miles in three days.

Herbert Hoover was an official employee of the U.S. Geological Survey this time, earning twenty dollars a month. The party had five horses, pack mules, and a cook who could make ham, Boston baked beans, and buckwheat cakes, Herbert wrote back to Dr. Branner.

One of the foreign geologists on the team had never seen a rattlesnake. One day Herbert found one near the trail and hit it on the head with a stick. He wrapped it in his bandana and hung it from the pommel of his saddle to take back to camp to show the foreigner. But on the way back to camp, the sun warmed the rattler and it woke up. Suddenly it sounded its alarm. Bert was scared, and the buzzing sound so close to the horse's ear was too much.

The horse reared up, threw Bert off into the brush, and took off at high speed. The snake dropped off and headed wherever snakes go at such times. Bert had to limp five miles back to camp. The incident did nothing to improve his love of horses.

"In these long mountain rides over trails and through brush," Bert later told Tad and May, "I finally arrived at the conclusion that a horse is one of the original mistakes of creation. He is too high off the ground for convenience and safety on mountain trails. It would have been better if he had been given a dozen legs so that he had the smooth and sure pace of a centipede.

"Furthermore, he should have had scales as protection against flies. And a larger water-tank, like a camel. All these gadgets were known to creation prior to the geologic period when the horse was evolved. Why were they not used?"

That summer Herbert also had his fill of mules. Since he was the youngest on the job, he was given the title of "disbursing officer." It took him a while to see this was no honor. He had to buy supplies and keep accurate records of all the money spent. One morning in the high Sierras, one of the pack mules, tied to a tree, was found dead of a broken neck.

Bert had to either pay for the mule or get two witnesses to say how the mule had died and swear to their story before a notary public. The witnesses decided that the mule had reached up with its hind foot to scratch behind its ear, and in doing so, it caught a loose shoe in the rope around its neck.

"Impossible," said the U.S. Geological Survey in Washington, and they charged Herbert Hoover sixty dollars for the dead mule.

Dr. Lindgren knew Bert needed every penny he earned, so he paid for the mule. And he raised Bert's pay to thirty dollars. But forever after, both Lindgren and Hoover watched mules and many times saw them scratching their heads with one hind foot.

Bert missed the first five weeks of his senior year because the job with Dr. Lindgren did not end on time.

"Please fix it somehow," Hoover wrote to Dr. Branner at Stanford.

Branner smiled. He could fix it with the school for Hoover to return late. He might even be able to fix Bert's condition in English that he had not yet worked off. But he intended to fix something else as well. He could hardly wait for his young assistant to return.

His first day back, Branner asked Hoover to help him teach his freshman geology class.

Dr. Branner had never before tried to play Cupid, but he thought he could not go far wrong this time. Everything about Lou Henry was perfect. She had sparkling, blue eyes and a broad grin that had a touch of Irish lilt in it. She loved camping, fishing, and hiking. She had even been born in Iowa. She was bright, well-educated, and fascinated with geology. In four years, she would become the first female geologist in the United States.

A tanned, muscular Herbert Hoover reported for the class. Then Branner sat back to watch the chemistry work.

Bert was staring straight into her blue eyes, but he was his usual silent self. He leaned on the lab table, looking casual, answering her questions with as few words as possible. If only the boy would talk or flirt or something, Branner groaned inwardly. He had no way of knowing that Lou had already turned Bert's knees to jelly and he was leaning on the table for support.

By Christmas, Bert and Lou were more than just casual friends.

"I have become a regular social swell," Herbert wrote to one of his friends back in Salem. "I have gone to every ball, and enjoyed myself better than ever before in my life."

Once again Dr. Branner was worried about Hoover. He would have to stop running the athletic programs, quit being the student body treasurer, and forget the campus elections in the spring. He was flunking German, had almost failed in

two other classes, and still had not passed the freshman English exam!

"You may be able to graduate all right," Branner told him, "but we are not turning out bachelors of art here. We are turning out geologists."

Bert did settle down and study hard. But the English professor was still not impressed. He said Hoover could not write a perfect paper without misspelled words and commas in the wrong place, and he should not graduate until he could.

A few days before graduation, Professor J. P. Smith handed Hoover one of the papers that he had written for his paleontology class.

"Mr. Hoover, I want you to rewrite this paper. Spell every word right, correct your grammar, and put all the commas in the right places!"

Bert did as he was told. Smith went over the paper and corrected all the errors Bert had missed.

"Now, copy it over perfectly," Smith ordered.

Later, at a faculty meeting, Smith read the paper and handed it to the English professor. The teachers agreed that Hoover deserved to graduate, since he was so unusually good in science. And the well-written paper did prove that the boy could express himself in written English. Dr. Branner and Professor Smith sighed with relief. It had been a close call.

The morning of May 29, 1895, Herbert Hoover was ready to graduate. Goodbyes were hard to say to so many good friends. Most of them were going home to find jobs. But Stanford had become Bert's home. No matter how far away life took him, he was going to look forward to returning again and again to this campus.

Clutching his diploma, Bert searched out the most important face in the audience of cheering friends. Lou Henry and Bert had an "understanding." But how long could he expect such a wonderful girl to wait for him? She had three more years of college. He had forty dollars in the whole world, and no job yet. And he was determined to help pay for Tad's college as Tad had helped him.

Just then the California sun shone down on the first graduating class of the new university. Herbert Hoover's old cheerfulness flooded back. Another way was about to open for him. Something else brand new that he had never tried before.

Whatever Happened to . . . ?

HOOVER, MAY. Herbert's little sister went to the State University of Oregon in 1892, and then to Friends Polytechnic School in Salem. In 1896, she and Cousin Harriett Miles moved to Oakland, California, to live with brothers Tad and Bert Hoover. They moved later to Berkeley, where May went to the high school to get credits to go to Stanford University. She married Van Ness Leavitt in 1899.

HOOVER, THEODORE. Tad went to Penn College in Oskaloosa, working again on the farm for Uncle Davis. In 1895 he went to work in the Tribune newspaper office in Oakland, California. Entered Stanford University in the summer of 1897. In 1901 he earned a degree in mining engineering. In June 1899, Tad married his childhood sweetheart, Mildred Crew Brooke. (Before she was adopted, she was Millie Branson—the object of Tad's devotion at the West Branch meetinghouse.) After World War I, he taught in the engineering department at Stanford, becoming the Dean of the College of Engineering. He retired in 1941 to his country home near Davenport, California.

HOUSE OF THE MAPLES. The home the Hoovers owned when Hulda died was sold after her death and is no longer standing.

LITTLE BROWN HOUSE. The small house where Hoover was born was rescued by the Hoover family after it had become a hamburger stand. Painted white and carefully restored by the National Park Service, it has among its furnishings Hoover's own high chair and his cradle made by his father. Also in West Branch you may visit the rebuilt BLACKSMITH SHOP, the SCHOOLHOUSE, and the restored QUAKER MEETINGHOUSE. In the small, reconstructed village are other houses of West Branch in the 1880s.

MILES, AGNES. Aunt Agnes, wife of Laban, lined up her children one day after World War I, saying, "I have something to say to thee. Our nephew and cousin now is one of the great men of the country and of the world. I do not believe it is proper for us to do anything or say anything that would imply familiarity. So I ask thee all never to refer to him again as Bert. He is to be Mr. Hoover or Herbert Hoover."

When Agnes passed away in Pawhuska, Oklahoma, the Osage chief, Lookout, and his wife came to her funeral in Indian costume to chant. They wanted to introduce her spirit to the Great Spirit, so that, if some day in paradise she had wandered away because she heard a child calling, He would care for her.

MILES, MAJOR LABAN J. Uncle Laban lived in Pawhuska the rest of his days, still working to improve the Indians' conditions. A serious case of pneumonia at age 84 kept him from going to Herbert Hoover's Presidential Inauguration.

OSAGE AGENCY. The agency became the town of Pawhuska when, in 1906, Congress passed the Allotment Act, which allowed lots to be sold to whites as well as Indians. In less than twenty years, the population grew from 2,000 to over 10,000. Pawhuska is now the county seat of Osage County.

OSAGE INDIANS. The Osage Indians came to Oklahoma from Kansas in September 1872, but not by choice. They had been moved farther west by "civilization." After the Allotment Act of 1906, the Indians were no longer able to roam the reservation as they pleased. They received $25,000 for sale of lands they had considered theirs. Oil was discovered on their land, making them among the richest of the Indians pushed onto reservations. Three villages formed after 1906 were Pawhuska (formerly Osage Agency), Hominy, and Grayhorse. Today these villages hold ceremonial war dances every year in June.

Herbert Hoover: The Man

1895   Whatever his dreams may have been on the day he graduated from Stanford University, Herbert Hoover's future did not get off to a brilliant start. The only job he could find was the lowliest and dirtiest in a mine— at two dollars a day. Yet it gave him knowledge of mining and of the men who did the dirty work that he could have learned no other way.

1896   Herbert, Tad, and May Hoover lived together in Berkeley, California, under the same roof for the first time since their mother had died. Cousin Harriett Miles lived with them. Herbert was hired by a mining engineer, Louis Janin, to be a lowly copyist, but he told Lou Henry that at least he "had his foot in the door" of an important company.

1897   Janin discovered that his employee Herbert Hoover had unusual talents in the mining field. He sent Hoover to Bewick, Moreing & Company in London, and they sent him to Australia to inspect gold mines. Hoover became manager of the Sons of Gwalia gold mine at $10,000 a year.

1899   The company next sent Hoover to help manage the Celestial Mines in China. He cabled Lou Henry in

California to ask her to marry him. She agreed at once, and they were married on February 10 in California. The next day, they sailed to China, unaware that a serious rebellion was brewing between the young emperor of China and his mother.

1900   The Chinese said that Hoover had "green eyes that can see through the earth and rock and find gold there." But in June the Hoovers and other "foreigners" were trapped under seige in Peking during the Boxer Rebellion. Hoover organized the food supplies to keep 380 foreign refugees, including eighty Americans, from starvation while 6,000 shells were fired into their section of the city. They were rescued by American Marines, and the Hoovers sailed to London in July.

1901   Hoover returned to Shanghai; Lou was in Japan. By the end of the year, Hoover's name was big in the mining world. He became a junior partner of Bewick, Moreing & Co. In the next seven years, the Hoovers had two sons and went around the world eight times. Herbert, Jr. was born in London in 1903, and Alan in London in 1907.

1907   The Hoovers built a six-room cottage in Palo Alto, next to Stanford University. They translated a medieval manuscript, *De Re Metallica*, from the Latin, and for fun even visited the sites of the ancient mines.

1909   Hoover lectured at Stanford and Columbia universities. He published his *Principles of Mining*. A few years later, he was invited to be on the Board of Trustees at Stanford.

1914   The Hoovers were in London on June 28 when an
         assassin's bullet started the First World War. The U.S.
         consul general asked Hoover to help get 200,000
         stranded Americans home. In the process, he learned
         that millions of Belgian and French children were
         starving because of the German invasions and the
         blockades by Allied ships.

         Hoover was momentarily torn at this time between
         making a fortune in his profession as a mining engineer
         or going into public service. From the day he decided
         on public service, he never took one dollar in payment.
         Even his salaries in later years as secretary of commerce
         and President, went into a fund for charitable causes.

         During the war, Hoover crossed the heavily mined
         English Channel forty times, dodging German U-boats.
         He asked the Germans not to sink food ships going to
         occupied countries, and they agreed until 1917. The
         Commission for Relief in Belgium (CRB) transported
         five million tons of concentrated foods to starving ci-
         vilians.

1917   The United States entered the war on April 6. Hoover
         returned to the U.S. to head the U.S. Food Admin-
         istration, an organization formed to make certain that
         Americans would have enough to eat. After the Ar-
         mistice in November 1917, Hoover returned to Europe
         to help find food for the starving women and children
         in much of Western Europe and the Middle East. He
         was criticized often for "feeding the enemy," but Hoo-
         ver always believed that the four-month delay in get-
         ting proper nourishment to the German children was
         what caused that generation to support Adolf Hitler
         later.

1919   The peace treaty that ended World War I was signed.

But Woodrow Wilson, President of the U.S., was ill and did not listen when Hoover warned him about certain aspects of the treaty that would cause trouble later. Everywhere Hoover went, he was honored. Belgian King Albert heard that Hoover disliked medals because they were military awards, so the king had an award, called "Friend of the Belgian People," a medal created just for Hoover. In Poland, 50,000 school children gathered in the streets to cheer the man who had fed them. In Finland, a new word was invented—"Hooveri." It means "deeds of benevolence." Women in many lands took empty flour sacks, embroidered them with lovely designs of flowers and thank-yous, and sent them to the Hoovers.

Meanwhile, Hoover took special care that the records of the war so recently fought were kept together. Later they formed the basis for the Hoover Institution of War, Revolution, and Peace that was dedicated at Stanford University in June 1941.

In September, Hoover returned to his cottage in Palo Alto. He opened an engineering office, bought an automobile, and took his family camping and fishing.

In October, President Wilson asked Hoover to entertain the king and queen of Belgium and their staff of thirty-eight people at his "estate," not knowing that Hoover's estate was a six-room cottage. But Hoover rented two estates in Santa Barbara and entertained the royal party. The Hoovers began building their "dream house" on the campus of Stanford University soon after.

1920   Hoover was put up for nomination at the Republican Convention as a candidate for President of the U.S., but Senator Warren G. Harding won the nomination.

Hoover became secretary of commerce. Hunger was still a world problem. Hoover began a series of "Invisible Guest" dinners, setting a tin plate at one place to represent a hungry child. At one dinner, he raised three million dollars that he sent to the European Relief Council.

1922   Hoover published his book *American Individualism*. Lou had become the president of the Girl Scouts of America. Herbert, Jr. went off to Stanford.

1923   Hoover went to Alaska with President Warren Harding. The President had a heart attack and died on the trip home. The Teapot Dome Scandal rocked Washington and the nation.

1929   Hoover became President of the U.S., taking his oath of office in March. On the reviewing stand was his old teacher who had once asked to adopt him, Mollie Brown Carran. Absent was Uncle Laban Miles, who was too ill to attend the ceremonies.

    In October the stock market crash was followed by the start of the country's worst depression. Unluckily, many people remember Hoover's presidency for those two disasters. Hoover tried to ignore the many attacks on him by the newspapers and by politicians. But he was not a politician. For so many years while growing up, he had taken blame for what was not truly his fault, biting his lip, and not answering back, that now he was unable to fight back. The smear campaigns hurt. Because he kept his private life entirely out of the public eye, many Americans felt that he was cold and unapproachable.

1933   Franklin Delano Roosevelt became President of the U.S. The Hoovers moved back home to Stanford. Herbert began to write his book *The Challenge to Liberty* and his *Memoirs*. He kept an apartment in New York's Waldorf Towers. The attacks on him continued, even to changing the name of Hoover Dam to "Boulder Dam" and not even inviting him to the dedication ceremony. (In 1947, an act of Congress changed the name back to Hoover Dam.)

1938   Hoover returned to Europe. He paid a visit to Hitler, but only four days later the fuehrer's troops invaded Austria. Hoover could see that war was ahead and he tried hard to keep the U.S. out of it. He tried to set up relief commissions to provide food for the civilians of Poland and Finland, but the war progressed too fast. One country after another fell to the German armies.

     In his efforts to provide food and medical supplies through commissions, Hoover made speeches and wrote articles on how to conserve food and how to distribute supplies to those in need. And he worked on the peace to come by publishing *Problems of Lasting Peace* in 1942. But he was getting older, and it was very hard for a peaceful person to be heard in a country that was arming for war.

1944   Lou Henry Hoover died in New York of heart failure.

1946   After the war, President Harry S. Truman asked Hoover to make a survey of the world's food supplies and to study the economic conditions in Germany, Austria, the rest of Europe, and also South and Central America. Hoover logged over 50,000 miles on that trip.

1962   On his eighty-eighth birthday, Hoover was in West Branch, Iowa, for the dedication of the Herbert Hoover Presidential Library.

1964   At age ninety, Hoover had not yet retired. He was working on a three-volume history of Soviet American relations, called *Freedom Betrayed.*

He died on October 20 and was buried in West Branch next to his beloved Lou.

Bibliography

Dennis, Ruth. *The Homes of the Hoovers*. West Branch, Iowa: Herbert Hoover Presidential Library Association, 1986.

Emery, Anne. *American Friend: Herbert Hoover*. Chicago: Rand McNally, 1967.

Hoover, Herbert. Nichols, William, editor. *On Growing Up*. New York: William Morrow, 1962.

Hoover, Herbert. *The Memoirs of Herbert Hoover: Years of Adventure, 1874–1920*. New York: MacMillan, 1952.

———. *The Memoirs of Herbert Hoover: The Cabinet & The Presidency. 1920–1933*. New York: MacMillan, 1952.

———. *The Memoirs of Herbert Hoover: The Great Depression, 1929–1941*. New York: MacMillan, 1952.

Irwin, Will. *Herbert Hoover: A Reminiscent Biography*. New York: Century, 1928.

Lane, Rose Wilder. *The Making of Herbert Hoover*. New York: Century, 1920.

Lyons, Eugene. *Herbert Hoover: A Biography*. Garden City: Doubleday, 1964.

Manuscripts (unpublished) written by Theodore Hoover, Harriett Miles, Laban Miles, Mary Agnes Minthorn, Henry John Minthorn, Elmer Edson Washburn, and unpublished diary of Archibald Crosbie.

Mathews, John Joseph. *Wah'Kon Tah*. Introduction by Maj. Laban J. Miles. Norman, Oklahoma: University of Oklahoma Press, ca. 1932. Second printing, 1968.

Nash, George H. *The Life of Herbert Hoover: The Engineer, 1874–1914*. New York: W. W. Norton Company, 1983.

Newspapers:
Kansas City Star, articles on Hoover
The Oregon Statesman, several copies 1889
West Branch (Iowa) *Times* and *West Branch Local Record*, 1874 to 1885.

About the Author

Investigating Herbert Hoover's childhood world gave Suzanne Hilton her first chance to visit Iowa. There she spent many hours in the Herbert Hoover Presidential Library at West Branch, reading old newspapers, diaries, letters, and journals, and collecting photos and drawings of homes and scenes of Bert's early years.

Only when she is deep in research or talking about history and genealogy is this author of fourteen books for young people truly happy. Her avid curiosity about details of long-ago everyday life and her vivid sense of historical times were fostered at Chatham College in Pittsburgh and Beaver College near Philadelphia, where she received her B.A., and, recently, recognition as a distinguished alumna.

When she is not working away at her word processor, Suzanne Hilton is out speaking to groups of young people and adults about her favorite subjects. Her lifelong hobbies include sailing, camping and photography.

About the Artist

As an illustrator and graphic artist, Deborah Steins has developed and illustrated advertising and done package and ad design for agencies as well as book and magazine publishers, ranging from trade show displays to puzzle books and retail packaging of storybooks. Her work has appeared in *Field & Stream* magazine, *Alfred Hitchcock's Mystery Magazine*, and other leading publications.

An alumna of the School of Visual Arts in N.Y.C., Deborah Steins has exhibited her work in the Master Eagle Gallery and Doubletree Gallery. Her paintings and drawings hang in private residences across the country.

Index